Into the Unknown:
Life Is So Much More than the Daily Grind

By Michael Carroll

Play More Better Press   Taos, New Mexico

Copyright © 2017 by Michael Carroll

All rights reserved. No part of this book may be reproduced or transmitted in any form or by any means, electronic or mechanical, including photocopying, recording, or by any information storage and retrieval system, without permission in writing from the author.

Contact the author at:
mcc@newmex.com

This edition was prepared for publication by
Ghost River Images
5350 East Fourth Street
Tucson, Arizona 85711
www.ghostriverimages.com

Manuscript preparation and cover art by Kit Lynch
kitlynch@taosnet.com

Cover design by Caryn Reardon
taosranch@gmail.com

Edited by Sarah Aschenbach
Inspired Solutions LLC
saasch@aol.com

ISBN 978-0-9991992-0-6

Library of Congress Control Number: 2017910859

Printed in the United States of America
July 2017

Table of Contents

Acknowledgements 5

Chapter 1: 7
    Trained Beliefs 7
    Television 7
    Earning Money 9
    The War and the Draft 11
    Dyslexia 11
    Pole Vaulting 13
    First Jobs 16
    Let Loose in the World 18
    The Draft—Piloting an Unknown River 20

Chapter 2: 25
    Searching 25
    Losing My Relationship Virginity 25
    Chasing Dreams 28
    The Voice 30

Chapter 3: 35
    The Army 35

Chapter 4: 49
    Conscientious Objection 49

Chapter 5: 69
    Everything is Within 69

Chapter 6: 83
    After the Light - Heading South 83

Chapter 7: 103
    Herman and Taos 103
    The Guru 104
    Transmuting the Personality 105
    Disillusionment 109
    The Guru Crosses the Rainbow Bridge 112

Chapter 8: 115
    Time to Rest, Assimilate, and Play 115
    Talking without Talking 115
    The Swift Currents of the Harmonic Convergence 117
    Mother Nature Heals 118
    Take Time to Play Canyon 120
    Rebirthing 121
    Revisiting Past Wounds 123

Chapter 9: 127
    Shamanism and the Medicine Wheel 127
    Journeying 128
    The Medicine Wheel 129
    Vision Quest 131

Chapter 10: 139
    Divorce Canyon and the Medicine Shield 139
    The Medicine Shield 141
    Healing Touch 142
    Dreaming My Shield 144
    Rooting My Personal Power 147

Chapter 11: 149
    The Unburied Shield 149
    Shamanic Retreat in Chiapas, Mexico 150
    Learning Native Council Ways 151
    Apprentice Training in Mexico 152
    The Hole 153
    Forty-Eight Hours in the Hole 155
    Deborah and the Garden of Eden 156
    Commitment 156
    A Silent War in the Mayan Lands 159
    Journeying in the Hole 161
    A Clash of Purposes 163
    Seeing a Bigger Picture 164
    Ending My Time with the Shaman 167
    Grandmother: A Crystal Medicine Woman 168
    More Intrigue 169
    Deborah Reappears 171

Chapter 12: 173
    Body Work - The Issue Is in the Tissue 173
    Deep-Tissue Work with Bryan Honda 174
    Isolating and Detaching from Pain 175
    Proper Breathing 177
    Martial Arts 178
    The Way of No Way 178

Chapter 13: 181
    Universal Law and Soul Development 181
    The Purpose of Spiritual Work 181
    Attuning to the Subtle Currents 182
    Universal Law 185
    How Does Universal Law Work? 186
    Soul Development and Reincarnation 187
    Early Childhood Souls (The first hundred or so lifetimes) 188
    Grade School Souls (the second hundred lifetimes or so) 190
    Teenage Souls (the third hundred lifetimes or so) 191
    Teenage Souls and the Manifestation of Desires 192
    Advanced Souls (the fourth and fifth hundred lifetimes or so) 193

About the Author 209

Acknowledgements

To my wife, best play mate and friend on the deepest levels Deborah Anderson for her love and encouragement to write this story.

To my niece Katie Carroll, for her early wisdom in telling me I need to be brutally honest in writing my memoir and highlighting the need to maintain a thread throughout the story

To my wonderful friend and Artist Kit Lynch for the willingness to clean up and prepare my manuscript for the final editor, for suggesting I contact Mike and Tama White as the self-publisher guides and for suggesting her magical pastel of the Rio Grande River Gorge as my book cover.

To a very talented artist/graph designer friend Caryn Reardon for designing and formatting Kit's pastel into the book cover.

To my brothers and sisters over the years ...Mark, Patric, David, Pam, Bob, Sue, Tim, Jeff, Maria, Bernie, Marybeth, Rick, Juana, Jack, Kim, Eric, Lou Ann, Michael, Kathy, Norbert, Shari, Susan, Tim, Leslie, Stewart, Dahvee, Charles, Roy, Larry, Douglas, Stephen, Nack, Kathi, Pat, Brian, Doug, Steve, Scott, Barbara, Wayne, Tommy, Walt and others.

To my camping and disc golf buddies in Taos and Pagosa Springs for keeping "Outdoor Play Time" with friends, vibrantly alive in our 50's 60's 70's

To my teachers along the way, in physical form and through the wisdom of the written word

To Mark Pritchard, Eric Larson and Ariana Kramer for reading and making constructive comments on my manuscript

To Sarah Aschenbach (final editor). For her wisdom to understand and articulate my story, for asking deep questions to help clarify what I was attempting to say.

To my brothers Dennis, Tommy, Walter and daughters, Amanda, Michelle, Jessica

I am most grateful for sharing sections of this life's river with you

Chapter 1:
TRAINED BELIEFS

Eternal hell is where I, Catholic third-grader Michael Carroll, would go. The nun was clear on that. That is, if I died with a mortal sin on my soul. Sins such as missing Sunday Mass or eating meat on Friday needed to be confessed to in order to avoid a fiery eternity.

Even at the tender age of eight, it was clear that God couldn't be like that. Although we didn't know it at the time, it was a man-made rule that used fear to control the masses. If someone in 2015 told you that you would go to hell for eating meat on Friday, you would think that they were crazy. Yet, back in 1961, this was a standard teaching of the Catholic Church.

This is just one minor example of the many ways we are indoctrinated into the beliefs of our materialistic and limited religious culture.

Television

This same year, the United States population of 183 million dove into the new world of television. Families were easy to support in the expanding economy. The resulting expendable income and leisure time resulted in many hours spent watching black-and-white images projected through the tube.

ABC, CBS, and NBC planned their programming to perfectly

coincide with the average family routine. On Saturdays, the television babysat kids with *Rocky and Bullwinkle* while their folks slept in. Most women still stayed at home raising the kids, and early afternoons featured daytime soap operas with continuing addictive stories. These shows, such as *The Edge of Night* and *As the World Turns* were timed perfectly so Mom could chill between morning chores and when the kids came home. The kids were immediately sucked in with afterschool programming before dinner. After dinner, parents watched local and national news while the kids did their homework. Then, by prime time—seven-thirty—the whole family gathered to watch shows such as *Flipper, Sea Hunt, Bonanza, I Dream of Jeannie, Combat, The Lone Ranger* or *The Beverly Hillbillies*. It is estimated that during this period, 85 - 90 percent of American homes owned a television.

Even so, my friends and I played outside any chance we could. I never considered watching television after school unless the weather prevented outdoor play. In the winter, we played until sunset, and in my home, this meant getting home early enough to watch television while my parents had their usual cocktails before dinner.

On the serious side, television was a powerful tool for communicating the political moves of the time. It was early in the year 1961 that President Dwight Eisenhower made his famous "Live Broadcasted Farewell Address" directly into the homes of the American people. In this ten-minute speech, he warned the American people of the rising "military-industrial complex." Reflecting back, I do not remember hearing a word about such a warning from him until after the year 2000.

Skip ahead to November 22, 1963, when President Kennedy was assassinated. With instant television coverage, the whole country watched every detail. In my lifetime, this marked the first major event to shock and traumatize the entire nation's mental and emotional consciousness in a matter of mere hours. The Warren Commission was formed to investigate the assassination and concluded that President Kennedy was assassinated by Lee Harvey Oswald, acting alone, and that Jack Ruby, who assassinated Oswald before he could stand trial, also acted alone.

This was the time in our lives when most people still believed that the news and the advertisements they saw and heard on television were true. Never do I remember anyone doubting the news. Generally speaking, people trusted news programs just as we trusted the teachings of the Church. We had no reason to doubt the honesty of our government. We didn't know that government officials fed the "proper" story to the three major television stations; in essence, this means that the government controlled the supply of information to the nation. False information was even used to sway the country into war, as when President Johnson lied to the nation about the Gulf of Tonkin incident.

These world events took place when I was in sixth grade and my first year in public school. The Catholic school I attended through fifth grade required me to wear a uniform, whereas in public school, I could wear whatever I wanted within certain limits, of course. This was a big change in my perception and personal expression.

Somewhere between my thirteenth and fourteenth birthdays, I became aware of a new feeling moving through my body. As it turned out, this feeling was natural to everyone. But I have to ask why not one person ever spoke about it to me beforehand. I had three older brothers and a dad who spoke not a single word about the physical sexual energy I would one day experience.

Earning Money

When I was twelve, I started to earn money. For fifty cents, I raked the stray stones from the yard back onto our driveway. For a few weekends, I worked at the local deli for seventy-five cents an hour until the boss realized I wasn't cut out for it. Always, in the winter, we boys shoveled driveways and walkways in the housing development for a dollar or two, depending on how deep the snow was. In the summer, there was my friend Wayne Elmore's father Charlie, who had roots somewhere in central Pennsylvania. He was a thin man with no teeth who worked the three to eleven shift at a local factory. Often he took us fishing at night. Charlie would get home from work, eat dinner, and then wake Wayne and me up sometime around midnight to fish the Passaic River with kerosene lanterns. The first fish I caught while night fishing was a twenty-seven inch freshwater eel. Once it was landed, Charlie got his foot behind the head of the eel and pinned it to the ground as if it were a biting snake in order to get the hook out of its mouth. He placed it in the bucket. A few hours later, we packed up. On the way home, Charlie stopped by the factory and gave his black co-workers our night's catch. The Blacks ate the eels, carp, and catfish from the Passaic, while we never even considered doing that, as the river was well known to be polluted.

Charlie wore many hats. In addition to being a factory worker, he was a small-animal taxidermist and ran a part-time landscaping business, too. His two part-time businesses provided the opportunity for Wayne and me to make a little money on the side. If we found a dead animal that was hit by a car, we would look it over carefully to make sure it was still fresh and in good enough condition for Charlie to stuff. If we were lucky, a chipmunk would get us thirty-five cents, a squirrel fifty cents, and a raccoon up to five dollars, but that was rare. Cutting grass was another way to make a few dollars on a Saturday. Around the Fourth of July one year, I accepted firecrackers as payment from Charlie instead of cash. I loved the deal, but my parents did not!

In June of 1966, the last full day of school was most memorable to me. We were called to the gym auditorium to practice receiving our grade-school diplomas. While walking down the hall towards the gym, I saw a few boys in the principal's office. They were the ones who got the feared "Repeat Eighth Grade" notice. When I got to the gym, my first steady girlfriend, Cathy, was crying because she thought I had gotten left back. It was very sweet of her, but once again, as a nun had once told me, I had passed narrowly.

It was 1967, and I was a freshman at Passaic Valley Regional High School. Its student body of two thousand resulted from combining kids from the three surrounding towns of West Paterson, Totowa, and Little Falls. Racial tensions in the nation were boiling, and the Vietnam War was in the process of escalating to over five hundred thousand combat troops.

The War and the Draft

My brother Dennis was beginning his fourth year as a public school art teacher when he was drafted. At the time, he was one month shy of turning twenty-six, which happened to be the age at which a young man could no longer be drafted. Dennis was sent to Vietnam in 1968. During his tour of duty, a neighbor's son, an older boy I had camped and fished with frequently, was killed in the war. Hatchie was the first young person I knew who had died. The family requested that parents of sons presently in Vietnam not go to the funeral, thus we as a family did not attend the memorial service. Afterwards, I heard it was very emotional. At the time, I did not know what "very emotional" was. Only now, fifty years later, do I wonder what I would have felt if I had attended that service?

Dennis made it home safely in the spring of 1969. To the best of my understanding, he never had to use his weapon. Luckily, he had been stationed in a relatively safe zone in Vietnam. The army was smart enough to recognize Dennis's skills as a teacher—or perhaps as highly skilled in the art of typing on an old-fashioned typewriter. He was ordered to report to work at army headquarters. However, I do remember seeing his photos of bombs going off in the distance, and there was a time near the end of his tour that he was required to carry his weapon everywhere.

Back at home, anticipating the return of their son from Vietnam, my parents purchased a bottle of champagne every week during Dennis's deployment overseas. Upon his return, Cousin Carol Walter and I greeted Dennis at the airport as he got off the plane. It was some weeks later when Mom and Dad had the big welcome home party with all the friends and relatives. Outside, the champagne corks were flying into the evening sky while I was enjoying my parents' blessing to get drunk.

Dyslexia

Life was good, except that I had to deal with being dyslexic. Back in the 1950s and 60s, there was no name for it, no special teachers or classes for the kids who had a hard time learning to read and spell. In

Catholic school, we were considered "slow" and often seated in the back of the class or in the row along the windows. Why was that? It was to make it easier for the nun to teach the kids who were able to pay attention and understand what she was saying in the normal way. The unspoken rule was, as long as we didn't make noise and distract the class, we were left alone to look out the window or, in my case, if it was springtime, to daydream about playing baseball or going fishing after school.

There were times when a nun punished me for distracting behavior. She would tell me to stand up, walk to the corner, and put my face into it; or, sometimes, I had to stand up and put my face to the blackboard, or sit on the floor next to her desk. On a few occasions, my actions in the classroom got me assigned to detention after school. I can remember my first time in detention. The boys from all grades who had been assigned to detention were held after school in the classroom closest to the principal's office. My clearest memory was of being in this class for the first time with fifteen to twenty older boys, and no girls. The nun sitting at the desk watching over us got up for a moment and walked into the hall to speak with another nun. The instant she left the room, every boy in the classroom lifted his hand up high and gave the nun the middle finger. Then, by the time we were released, all the buses were gone. Not knowing any of the older boys or the parents who were picking them up, I had to walk the three miles home alone for the first time while lugging my book bag. No wonder those boys had given her the finger!

From the time I started school, my grades were on the edge of failing. Fs were not uncommon in the subjects of reading, writing, history, geography, and so on. In other words, any schoolwork requiring reading, writing, spelling, or remembering what I had read was a painful experience.

There was no word for dyslexic children in my day. But nowadays, we know that, according to 2015 statistics, dyslexic kids represent 20 percent of the student population and that, within that 20 percent, there exists a wide range in its degree of severity. My high school grade point average after four full years was a solid 1.6. How did I manage?

Attitudes develop early as survival tools for the personality. In my memory, no one in my family gave me a difficult time about getting poor grades. I can also remember the nun telling my mother, "Keep Michael in after school and force him to study!" My mother's flat-out response was, "I will not take away Michael's playtime."

Other boys were not so lucky. Their families were telling them that they were stupid. They were forced to study. But you can't force a dyslexic kid to study. It just doesn't work that way. Behavioral problems develop when a child's life is void of anyone with basic understanding of the condition.

Pole Vaulting

Outdoor activities soothed my spirit: playing on the ball field, in the woods, or down by the river; running track in high school. School grades didn't matter in track, unless, of course, your grade point average was below a 1.0. At 1.6, I did not fear becoming ineligible for sports. The straight As in gym and shop classes kept my GPA high enough to coast above the failing line.

The spring of my junior year was a very good time. I passed my driver's license test, purchased my first car, and broke the high school pole-vaulting record that had stood at 11 feet, 8 inches. It was after school in late May or early June when our school had an away track meet at Ridgewood, NJ. Before this meet, my previous best height at pole vaulting was 11 feet, even. On this particular day, I won the competition at and earned the right to choose the next height of the bar. Without hesitation, I set it at 11 feet, 9 inches. I ran down the runway and planted the fiberglass pole in the pole box that sits in front of the foam landing pit. I leaned back and went up and over on my first try. The bar was raised to 12 feet, and the same thing happened, up and over. Next, I set the bar at 12 feet, 6 inches. Again, up and over.

Thirteen feet was the obvious next height. It was then that I looked around and noticed that all the other track and field events of the day had been completed, and most of both track teams had gathered around the pole vault to see me go over 12 feet, 6 inches. But the magic spell of being totally out of my thought-mind, where the body did what it needed to do without thinking about it, had broken, and I missed three attempts at 13 feet. Even so, I was elated. In a matter of twenty minutes, I had risen to glory as an athlete.

I was so enthralled by pole vaulting that during the "Summer of Love" in 1969, I was completely unaware of weed, LSD, Woodstock, or the anti-war peace and love movement that was sweeping the nation. My focus early during that summer vacation was on attending a week-long, pole-vaulting camp in eastern Pennsylvania, where the head instructor was the first college student to vault over 16 feet. I was the only kid who actually drove his car to the camp, and upon my arrival, they took my car keys. We were housed in group cabins in the woods near a lake. There was no quarter-mile track for pole vaulting, so we used the summer camp's paved outdoor basketball court as the runway. It was long enough and worked perfectly fine. They trained us hard, and on the last day, we had a competition. The best guy went over 13 feet, and I came in second by clearing 12 feet. From my point of view, camp was over. I had no need to spend one more night just to get a trophy. I packed up, retrieved my car keys, and left before the ceremonies so that I could make it back home in time to hang out with the boys on a Friday night in late June.

In early July, I got a call from someone who worked at the Totowa community pool, who asked if I would be interested in working as a lifeguard for the rest of the summer. Yes, of course!

By the fall of my senior year, I was all pumped up to run cross-country with the idea that it would help me continue my training for pole-vaulting season in the spring. However, I kept getting sick every other week with a sore throat and fever until the doctor said, "One more time, and the tonsils are coming out!" That one more time happened, and near the end of October of 1969, I spent two days in the hospital. The first night was easy. That was before the operation. Early the next morning, I remember two things clearly. Number one, a big, hefty nurse walked into my room and told me she was there to give me an enema in preparation for surgery. Talk about getting blindsided without warning! I knew what an enema was, but I had never had one. There I was, bent over in the bathroom, as this lady stuck a Vaseline-covered tube up my butt. She said, "Let me know when you've had enough."

About a second after she let the water run into my butt, I said, "Enough!"

"Oh, come on, honey," she said, "you need to take a little more than that."

So I did, and she stopped the next time I said, "Enough." After that, I got a shot in the arm. Ten or fifteen minutes later, I was out in the halls, dancing! The nurse laughed, put me back in bed, and pulled the side bars up as a reminder not to get out. Thankfully, I stopped getting sick after the operation.

By spring, I was strong and focused. At the first track meet of the season, I upped my record to 12 feet 8 inches. A week later, I was fearless when I ran down the runway and planted the pole. My steps were perfect as the pole landed perfectly in the box. I leaned back and held on to the pole as the power from my speed and weight transferred into the pole. Normally the pole would bend just so far and then begin to lift me into the air. This time, however, when I leaned back, the pole bent so much that I was lying flat on my back on the runway before I started to go up. Instantly, I flashed that I had never been here before, and I had never seen anyone lean back so far yet actually ride the pole up and over. I let go of the pole and the next thing I knew, my coach was looking me in the face intently, and for the first time, I noticed that we were hosting an afterschool track meet. I drew a blank. Why were they there? Someone asked me if I remembered getting the record the week before, and I said no. Eventually my memory all came back, and the doctor gave be a clean bill of health.

The following week, I broke my ankle. By the time my ankle healed, it was only a few weeks before the state track meet. In June of 1970, at the New Jersey State regionals, I cleared 12 feet, 1 inch, along with one other guy. We agreed to raise the bar to 12 feet, 6 inches. I ran down the runway, planted my pole, leaned back as my weight transferred into the bend in the fiberglass pole, and then snap, the pole broke. In a flash, I tumbled forward through the air, and by the grace of the pole-vaulting gods, I landed safely on my back in the foam pit. There were no physical side effects, except that the pole I had been using for two years was gone. Worse, the trust I had always placed in any fiberglass pole was gone. A coach from a different school offered me the use of one of his poles. The pole was probably rated at 140 pounds, whereas the pole I broke was rated at 150 pounds. Without time to practice, I ran down the runway, planted the pole, and had to bail out of the jump so I wouldn't find myself holding on to the pole and lying on the pavement again. My high school track career was over.

I had suffered a number of track-related injuries in high school. I broke my foot freshman year when it landed on the edge of the wooden 2' x 6' frame holding the sawdust for the landing pit. In tenth grade, I developed the bad habit of banging my left knee against the pole on my way up, which eventually caused water on my knee. In eleventh grade, I hurt my back tossing the javelin and was lucky that my doctor knew chiropractic. Fortunately, I got through those years without any lasting physical problems.

First Jobs

West Paterson was the small town I grew up in. It was located about eighteen miles west of New York City. We could go a few miles and then merge onto a highway that led directly to the Lincoln Tunnel and downtown Manhattan. In the opposite direction was an intersection circle of highways that led to mountain lakes, ski areas, and the Playboy Club of Northern New Jersey. Driving west led to the Delaware River Water Gap National Recreation area, where we camped and fished.

The land south of the circle bordered the lowlands around the Passaic River and was swampland. This is the area that had the greatest impact on my life during the Sixties. On this acreage were the local drive-in theater and the outdoor ice-skating rink. On the land between them, the largest indoor mall in the nation was being constructed.

I continued to make money when I could. I had to wait until I was sixteen to work at a store legally and have taxes taken out of my paycheck. My first official job was at Goodies Hamburgers for $1.40 an hour. I often had to walk to and from work. My boss's name was Mr. B. For some reason, he took a liking to me—not in a sexual way—

but he trained me to work the register, clean the counter, take out the garbage, and clean around the outdoor garbage cans. I also came in early to prepare for the day by turning on the grill for the burgers and heating the oil for the fries. In those days, the french fries were fresh and made on the spot. We cleaned, chopped, and blanched the potatoes needed for just that day. The milkshakes in 1968 were made from real cream, and the machines were emptied and cleaned every night while the milkshake liquid was stored overnight in the walk-in icebox with the raw hamburgers.

Eventually I learned to be the cook, which paid $1.65 per hour. During the summer lunch rush, I could cook forty-eight hamburgers at once! At the time, burgers were 15 cents, or 20 cents with cheese. One hot summer night, the meat freezer died. Mr. B had me cook the burgers that had turned brown and stank! "Just sprinkle extra onions on them." We warned all our friends when they came to the window!

In late spring of 1969, I purchased my first car for $125.00. It was a white, four-door, 1961 Chrysler Newport that was built like a tank, had push buttons on the dash to change gears, and got poor gas mileage. In those days, two dollars put 7.1 gallons of gas in the tank. Driving allowed my friends and me to go on many exciting adventures! We would head into New York City or go sixty miles south to the Jersey Shore, the two happening places to be in our world.

My generation is the last to remember what it was like before the new Interstate 80 cut the boundary between our town and the City of Paterson, New Jersey. It was the route east to the George Washington Bridge or west to the circle near the mall, and then on to California. Until then, we boys in the neighborhood lived in innocence.

Wayne Elmore and I fished together a lot. However, if the carp weren't biting, we would cast our lines into the water, secure the poles so the big one wouldn't pull our rods and reels into the river, and find something else to do. These were the old days when Tarzan would swing on vines from tree to tree in the TV jungle. Imagine the fun when Wayne and I and a few others boys discovered vines growing from the trees down by the river! We soon figured out that, with a good running start, we could swing out over the Peckman, a small river in our town that flowed into the Passaic River.

Let Loose in the World

I graduated from high school in 1970, free to do or be whatever I wanted. I had been let loose by the times and culture into the winds of physical and economic survival. I could choose to go to college. I made plans to go to Paterson State College, but my 1.6 GPA was not high enough for general acceptance. Fortunately, my track coach called their track coach, and I was accepted because of my pole-vaulting abilities.

A few days after graduation, my friend Steve and I drove to Myrtle Beach for our first real adventure into the world. We had a total blast, swimming in the warm ocean water and meeting Southern girls. I still remember my first contact with a Southern girl, who said, "I can't hardly understand you, you Yankee dog, you!" Ten days later, we were back in Jersey, and I began my second summer of lifeguarding at the Totowa community swimming pool. It was late that first summer after high school that I first smoked weed in the back of a friend's parked, 1960, four-door pink Cadillac. We were smoking and listening to the song, "A Day in the Life" from the Beatles' Sgt. Pepper's Lonely Hearts Club Band when I realized I was high for the first time! It was a fun summer.

September was like every other September I'd had in my life. Its rhythm said, "Time to go to school." The first class I remember was English Lit 1. The professor said right up front, "If you can't pass my class, you shouldn't be in college." Not a good sign. I tried, but I flunked out by Christmas. I remember now that my mother made me pay the cost of tuition for that first semester because she knew I would flunk out. She didn't come right out and say it, but it was a lesson in, "If you want it, you have to pay for it."

Flunking out of college at Christmas had its rewards. No more school! Mom and Dad gave me permission to convert the basement's abandoned coal bin into my new bedroom. I needed a few pieces of sheetrock, which I found across the brook and woods in the still-expanding housing development. Wood pallets lifted the mattress off the cement floor so it didn't get wet when rains flooded the basement.

Into the Unknown

A scavenged carpet, a black light, and a stereo to play my albums completed my man cave.

For the first time in my life, I didn't have to go to school in the morning. I didn't need to worry about waking up early, so I spent most evenings with friends, getting stoned and listening to music. Friday night was every night. Unlike my brothers when they were my age, I could go in and out of the house through the basement door while Mom and Dad were asleep two floors above.

During that winter, Steve and I saved our money and made plans to visit Myrtle Beach for the month of May or possibly longer. When the time came, we drove south through the night and, by the next morning, we parked at the end of Ocean Boulevard where the road dead-ended at the state park. Exactly in this spot, we found a wonderful older lady who rented us one small room with two beds, which was perfect for our budget, and there we lived for the first extended time without Momma's good cooking. I clearly remember the pains and gas in my stomach after living for a month on Kool-Aid, coconut cookies, and the cheapest hotdogs and pot pies. It was a practical lesson on diet, which is something I had never even considered until then.

Upon returning in June, I learned the art of golf caddying at the local Jewish golf course for cash. Carrying two golf bags around the course for 18 holes paid sixteen dollars, or about four dollars an hour, which was a very good wage then. My life continued as a fun extension of my wonderful childhood, without school, and my evenings were free to do as I pleased.

Internally, I had no vision in my consciousness to guide my life in any particular direction. Yet, the rhythm of my twelve years of education had finally come to an end. It was now up to me to decide what my life would be. I had not experienced any desires, thoughts, or strong feelings to guide me on what to do with my life. No profession had ever grabbed my attention, like wanting to be a fireman or a doctor. Under my yearbook picture, I listed my dream as "To make a living as an athlete." I knew now that it would not be possible. Yes, my experience growing up had showed me that I was a very good athlete who had the ability to make the starting lineup in every sport I played, but there were always those few guys who rose above me to be the cream of the crop. Pole vaulting to 12 foot 8 set a record in my school, but there were one or two other guys in the state who could vault 13 to 13 foot, 6 inches. And in baseball, a guy named Ron Norman, who made it to triple A as a pitcher, always struck me out. So I knew I didn't have the right stuff to make money playing ball.

Perhaps because I couldn't read or comprehend books very well, I missed out on some of the imprinting that schools have on children, but I decided that there was more to life than working a full-time job every week. Getting high in the basement and listening to music was fun and exciting for awhile, but it had gotten old. The thrill of feeling and doing something new was gone. Stagnation is the word that comes to mind. But up until then, I had never experienced stagnation. How was I to know that it was slowly seeping into my life?

I can say that I never thought seriously about the future, and no one ever questioned me on my personal beliefs, and I mean no one. It was not until the ripe age of nineteen that the subject was ever raised.

The Draft—Piloting an Unknown River

On August 5, 1971, the military draft lottery number drawn for my April 24th birthday was 21. A few weeks later, my friend Walter Who, the guy with the pink Caddy, invited me on a trip with his sister and her New York friends. They had rented a remote cabin on a small lake about a hundred miles north of Ottawa in Canada.

We were in the wilds. At the cabin, one of the guys asked me about my plans and thoughts concerning my almost-certain induction into the army, and I didn't have an answer. I was speechless as he rattled my cage. Literally, he was the first person to challenge me to speak my truth. It was the first time, and it blew me away. I decided to walk down to the lakeshore in the darkness to be alone. I looked at the calm lake and saw the reflection of the stars, and when I looked up, there were so many stars that there was no space between them. The sky was alive and moving. Never again have I seen such a night sky.

Unexpectedly, I was moved by thoughts and emotions that I had never before encountered. How was I to explain this to myself? What was I to do? These feelings had carried me into an intense, uncharted experience. My river rafting experiences growing up came to mind. I felt like I was piloting a raft on an unknown river.

Back during the spring of 1967, we'd had an abundance of rain, and the two rivers in our town overflowed their banks. We boys got together and decided to build a raft and float on the smaller Peckman River until it merged downstream into the much larger Passaic River. We spent several days scavenging a few 55-gallon drums, boards, wood pallets, nails, and rope and building the raft. Pushing it into the Peckman River, using long sticks for poles, we began our journey at the exact spot where we had swung on vines a few years earlier. From there, the river meandered through thick woods. As we made our way around the bends and entered a long straightaway that resembled the entrance lane to a highway, our raft picked up speed.

First, we heard and then we saw that we were approaching the fork where the mighty Passaic meets our humble Peckman. The long sticks we held in our hands to navigate around the bends of the smaller river had become useless. The river deepened as the fast current from the larger river grabbed the 55-gallon drums as if they were empty plastic water bottles, hurtling down a desert arroyo during a flash flood.

The amplified vibration and powerful speed of the bigger river heightened our already over-stimulated senses. Now the main concern was keeping our balance. Nothing else mattered. The sticks that had been rendered useless for navigation became balancing poles, like those used in the circus for walking the tight rope. Our challenge was to maintain our balance while keeping our footing on the wobbly wood raft as it bobbed up and down on the swift, bumpy ripples. We were 100 percent focused. We had no time to freak out as our small river was fully absorbed by the muddy Passaic. Up ahead, the river bent slowly to the right. We boys were in our full glory, whooping in excitement. However, change can happen in moments, and the heavy current pulled the raft to the river's center, where our raft-building and physical-balancing skills were tested to the limit. Luck plays a role in rafting, as it does in life, and we were blessed that the current slowly pushed us up against the opposite bank as the river straightened out.

We had landed on the Totowa side of the river without getting wet!

That very afternoon, we had pushed off with no clue as to where we would end up. We'd had no plan. We had never experienced a flood, and we had never built a raft. We'd had only two things going for us: we had built lots of tree forts and tree houses, and we were all very good swimmers. We were the boys who enjoyed challenging each other in holding-our-breath competitions, counting how many underwater pool laps we could complete before taking a breath. We did it just because we were teenage boys with the good intention of having an adventure.

We followed only one decree, which was so obvious to us that we didn't need to speak it aloud: we would never go under the bridge that divided West Paterson and Totowa from the city of Paterson. By 1967, the Passaic River had been placed on the list of most-polluted rivers in the country. We always knew enough not to eat the fish or drink the water. We also knew it would be better to abandon the raft and swim to shore in the cold, muddy water than to go under the bridge. Going under the bridge meant going into the dangers of the unknown.

Life seemed to have gone along quite nicely until the Paterson race riots erupted during the hot summer of 1964. The town's middle-class American shoppers evaporated, and Paterson's shopping areas dried up like the Earth with no rain. This was when our little town had given birth to one of the country's first big box stores, The Great Eastern Mills, which was conveniently placed on the westbound lane of Route 46. This store and the others that followed quickly diverted all the economic flow away from downtown Paterson. No consideration was given to the economic damage being done to the town of my father's birth. On the west side of white, Christian, middle-class Paterson, we knew that Paterson's economic woes were the fault of black people. "They moved in, and look what happened!" was a phrase we heard often.

Like so many things during the early Sixties, nothing of meaningful social importance was ever discussed in a fair and balanced manner. Never was a word spoken about the perspective of the blacks. Paterson was no longer the place my father had known. He had watched it change. We all watched the world change as our population expanded. Dad was an honorable guy, but he had a chip on his shoulder that I noticed from time to time. Was it because Paterson now triggered fear, blame, and resentment in many adults in the surrounding area? As teenagers, we heard only the negative stories, and were told to avoid Paterson when possible. We were told never to go under the bridge to the unknown.

Michael Carroll

Chapter 2:
SEARCHING

The stagnation I had been feeling started to move when my first internal vision occurred, right after returning from Canada. In it, I was floating in the middle of a big river on my personal, one-man raft. Looking around at the landscape, nothing looked familiar until I allowed my eyes to focus upstream upon a distant bridge. That's when I knew I had gone past the diving bridge of my childhood, the bridge that marked the boundary of everything I had been told and everything I had experienced or thought about life up to then.

Soon after returning from Canada, I visited the local Navy recruiting office with the idea of becoming a Navy Seal. The recruiter was gathering the papers for me to sign when we started discussing the length of service required to enter the Navy. The words "four-year tour of duty" ended the conversation on the spot. No way would I sign up for four years! I had never even considered four years. I had assumed it would be a two-year tour, like the army draft.

Losing My Relationship Virginity

After the experience at the recruiter's office, I needed to walk off some steam. In those days when we were upset, had nothing to do, the weather was bad, or we wanted to people-watch, we would go and walk around the Willow Brook Mall. The same day I left the recruiter, I met my first, new downstream-of-the-bridge friend, Carolyn. While cruising the mall, we noticed each other in passing and both kept looking back at each other until at last we stopped and introduced ourselves. I quickly forgot the Canadian guy's warning about the military in exchange for this female playmate.

Together, we drove into New York for concerts or visited Greenwich Village and listened to folk singers at the Dug Out. One evening, we got to ride in the back seat while friends drove us into the city. We took advantage of the situation by taking a pill to get us high and then smoked some weed. We were on our way to see Rod Stewart in Madison Square Garden when his hit song "Maggie May" was number one on the national charts. Everything was great until the noise from the warm-up band became too loud. In an arena that held 20,000, we were only a few rows below the highest seats in the venue. We were also directly facing the stage. The sound system looked a mile away, yet we were barraged by sound waves that came at us and then bounced back at us again off the back wall. Due to sensory overload, we looked at each other and knew we had to escape our seats. We found refuge on the walkway around the arena where the bathroom and concessions were. We walked for a time and then sat against the wall as people walked by. No one ever questioned us. We were just a little too high to deal with the concert as we, me as a nonsmoker, inhaled Marlboro cigarettes to pass the time. Several hours later, we had come down enough to go back to our seats for the last few songs, including "Maggie May."

My education process with Carolyn continued as we encountered a few of the more turbulent sections of the river. Once, we were riding the New York subway heading down to the village when I noticed that a big black man standing a few feet away was staring at me. It started to freak me a little. Then, when he reached into his jacket pocket, I thought maybe he had a gun, and I froze. The rat-a-tat of the rolling wheels of the subway car seemed to go on forever. Finally, it stopped, and the doors opened at our destination. We got up and walked out. The man never moved and never said a word or changed the expression on his face.

I also had intense experiences with Carolyn. We were down in the basement listening to the Fleetwood Mac album, Future Games, when an unexpected wave of deep sadness washed over me with such power that I started to cry. It was weird. I had never cried before out of sadness. Sure, I had cried as a kid when I didn't get my way or when I fell down and broke a bone or cut myself, but this was different. The wave didn't come from the external physical environment. It came from within me somewhere. It was all very strange. The emotional wave itself lasted for just one song and then dissipated, and we did not talk much about my being so distraught.

Carolyn confronted me about my depression as our close relationship was dissolving. We didn't fight or argue, but I got the message. It was too difficult to continue down the river together. Somehow, we had managed to make it through a dangerous stretch without getting killed. We were no longer relationship virgins, you might say, yet we still lacked experience and were both more than a little shaken up after surviving our first winter downstream from the dividing bridge. As a result, we disconnected the rope that connected our rafts and went our separate ways.

I was caught in an internal struggle. The current of my life had speeded up, and I was starting to feel uncomfortable about the clouded mystery of what might lie ahead. The fun and games quickly came to an end when I realized I had to deal with my own survival.

It was mid-winter of 1972. I no longer had a girlfriend, so I went back to hanging out with the gang from high school, the ones who smoked weed in the back of the pink caddy and who hadn't gone off to college. It didn't take long to realize that something was different. I knew what it was, sort of. I was not the same guy. The boys noticed it as well. I asked questions and tried to start somewhat serious conversations about life, but they would have nothing to do with it. I had become the weird guy. They hadn't gone past the dividing bridge. They were still blindly accepting what the culture was telling them without questioning anything. They weren't even aware of the option that you could think for yourself and choose a way of living and believing. So, to them, there was nothing to talk about. Once you go past the bridge, there is no going back. My hunger for truth and understanding was so encompassing that I knew I wouldn't be hanging with those guys, anymore.

Hoping for something new and inspiring to happen, I contacted my friend Bill from high school, who was still living at home while going to Seaton Hall University. In the past, Bill and I had run track and cross-country and played ball-golf together. He was also a year older, which was a plus for those of us seventeen or younger, because he could drive into New York City at eighteen and buy alcohol. Bill had also graduated in 1969, so it had been a good year or two since we had visited. Lots had happened over those years, including the fact that I now smoked pot almost every day. When Bill and I got together, the first thing I did was fire up a joint, and the first thing Bill said was, "Why do you want to smoke that joint?"

Shit, just like the time in Canada, I didn't have an answer. I felt numb and I couldn't see clearly. I wanted to know why I wasn't happy and why everyone all of a sudden seemed to be in a rut. We were going through the motions, waiting for life to happen. Everyone else knew that, didn't they?

It was mid-winter. The days were short, the nights long, and for the first time in my life, I struggled to keep my head above water mentally and emotionally. I was alone and dazed. I had no real idea where I was or what was happening around or within me. I was being carried through the turbulent water on a raft that was half-filled with air.

Chasing Dreams

It was toward the end of February or early March when the weather shifted. Breezes of spring energy filled the air, calling for a detour onto another river. Even though spring had once marked the beginning of baseball, fishing, and track, this energy in 1971 took Steve, Eddie, and me to Myrtle Beach for a weeks' stay at the state park to enjoy the early heat of the South and hang out on the beach with the waves. It was our luck that girls our age were camping in the spot next to ours. It was these girls who asked us Jersey Boys if we wanted to take a hit of acid and trip with them on the beach, watching the moon rise out of the ocean. Watch the moon rise out of the ocean and trip on acid? We had only heard about tripping up until that point in our lives, and to be honest, none of us had thought much about the moon or, for that matter, ever considered that the moon rose out of the ocean like the sun.

We took the hit of acid and walked to the beach. The sunset and the stars looked as they normally did until a few hours later, when the red, three-quarter moon rose out of the ocean. The acid I took must have been weak, because I wasn't nearly as excited as the girls, but overall, it was a pleasant experience.

A year later, Bill and I started making plans to drive south during the first week of April for another Spring Break getaway from New Jersey. My cousin Jimmy wanted to go, too. He also told us about a music festival that was to be held on the beach in the Bahamas. From the information we gathered, it was a three-day, outdoor music festival that would rival Woodstock. We all felt the dream! This was our opportunity to make up for what we had missed back in 1969. Dreaming and making plans for our trip had the unexpected side effect of breathing air into my raft. We decided to drive south to the Miami airport, buy plane tickets, and somehow get to the festival.

Bill and I had more free time than Jimmy, so we decided to drive to Myrtle Beach a few days earlier. The plan was for Jim to meet us at the state park, and from there we would all drive south to Miami in his new car. Jim arrived a little spaced and tired from driving the seven hundred miles straight through from Jersey to Myrtle Beach, so I got behind the wheel of his car and started the drive south to the Miami airport. We didn't call ahead to get prices on the airline tickets, and we never thought about where we would sleep. After driving a good part of a day and all night, we arrived at the Miami airport as the dawn was breaking through the dark night sky.

Fifteen minutes later, we walked out of the airport after realizing that there was no way we could afford to fly. The dream suddenly vanished. Poof, the festival was gone. We left the airport to find a place to have breakfast and discuss what to do. We took out the map and decided to drive further south to Key Largo. We imagined that this Florida Key would be like the beach and water scenes from the television show Flipper that we had watched growing up. Our dream of the rock concert turned to a dream of snorkeling in the clear, fish-filled waters of the Florida Keys. And when we'd had enough of that, we would soak up some rays on the beach.

Our new dreams did not match the reality on the ground, either. We discovered that the water was way too cold and the cost to rent a mask, fins, and snorkel wasn't worth it. We turned around to drive north along the coast until we found a beach filled with young people.

First stop was Miami Beach. As I remember it, the Atlantic coastline of Miami was filled with hotels. We drove by all the hotels and soon realized that even the cheap hotels on the beach were not in our budget, so we continued north in Jimmy's fire-engine-red Oldsmobile Cutlass Convertible. Everything was all new, unknown, and exciting.

When we reached Fort Lauderdale, our eyes lit up and our mouths were all big smiles. We had heard about Spring Break from movies like Where the Boys Are, and this was it. The sidewalk and beach were filled with thousands of people our age. There were no hotels blocking the beach from the road, and to top that off, an outdoor music stage was set up for live music later in the day. How much better could it get?

We found a place to park and walked toward the beach. We had just merged into the crowd when some guy sitting on the bumper of his car asked us if we wanted to buy some pure mescaline. He said one hit is mellow, and two hits are really nice. Oh, we had money in the budget for this!

The Voice

This was our first day at the beach after the long drive. There was no doubt now that the energy had shifted. It seemed that the winter months' underinflated raft had firmed up, and the turbulent waters had calmed down. For the first time in many months, I was able to see beyond my personal internal struggles and simply enjoy my surroundings. For sure, it had something to do with the shift between the congested suburbs of northeast Jersey and the warmth of a sandy south Florida beach filled with young people in bathing suits. But there was more to it than that. After I took the hit of mescaline, I heard a clear voice speaking to me from inside my consciousness. I know now, many years later, that what I now call the Voice was the same voice that others have referred to as "the clear calm voice within" or "the soul communicating with the personality."

On the beach and under the influence of a mind-altering drug, I became extremely curious as to what people were thinking and whether or not they were happy. For the first time, I was starting to explore beyond my own thoughts. When I asked people around me, "Are you happy?" everyone said they were, but it seemed to me that this was not 100 percent true. Many seemed to be just going through the motions. They were on the beach, and sure, that makes us naturally feel good, but had they gone under the bridge? That is, had they gone past the familiar? I was clearly seeing that very few had. That day was the most wonderful day internally than I had experienced in a very long time—if ever—and thus by the end of the day I declared it the best day of my life!

The next day I was still jazzed from the day before, and I decided that I needed to find out if I could keep feeling that good, but naturally. I was convinced that the experience of the day before was enhanced by taking a pill and equally convinced that the enhanced consciousness could be achieved without the pill.

My enthusiasm was high. I zipped through the day, seemly as high as the day before, but without the pill. By the end of the day, I was convinced that the second day was the best day of my life because I had done it naturally. I'd had two "best days of my life" in a row.

On the third day, I took two hits. The weather couldn't have been better, and even more people were walking the white-foam line between the ocean and the beach. It didn't take long to notice that the people walking the beach seemed happier than those who were not. They were more open and friendlier. Why? Was the thin, white line of foam a healing place to walk?

I was finding it easier to identify, by look and intuition, which individuals I could approach for conversation. I wonder now, were they people who had passed under the bridge? Some people on the beach stared off into the ocean, while others sat in circles, talking and smoking pot from a pipe carved out of a fresh apple. One thing for sure, everyone was being rejuvenated by Mother Nature after the long, northern winter.

I had a most wonderful experience on the beach, walking and talking with people. I was moving fast on the river of my life, but, for the moment, there were no rapids or boulders to avoid, and I felt very safe. The riverbanks were wide, and the water wasn't brown and cloudy like the Passaic. It was clear and user-friendly, like the Delaware River near the Water Gap in northwestern Jersey.

The music started late in the afternoon and continued until dark. I was still going strong and was near the stage when the last band of the evening said good night. What to do, now? During the evening, I had found two sticks that I could bang together to make a warm, clicking sound. When band signed off, I jumped up on the stage and started stick-clicking in front of the microphone until the sound was cut. I was still in full buzz.

I hadn't seen Jim or Bill for hours. They were somewhere among thousands, but I was in the flow, and it was easy to find my friends once I started looking for them.

Together, we walked back to Jimmy's new car. We decided we were not yet ready to drive, so we pushed the 8-track back into the deck and listened to the Moody Blues.

The two albums we listened to that night were The Question of Balance and The Threshold of a Dream. I had been listening to the Moody Blues almost exclusively for several months; their sounds and messages helped to lift my mood. But this night, my experience was more intense. The words penetrated my consciousness with such clarity that they lifted me out of the fog I had been in for my entire life. During this moment, my inner river flowed calm and strong, and it was clear enough that I could see the riverbed for the first time.

For me, life beyond the bridge had transcended the teachings of our culture.

During this time, no one understood my new concerns about life.

I felt very much alone in my thoughts and perceptions of the world. I began to develop a relationship with this inner voice as it offered an explanation for what was happening to me. The Voice said, "It's just like a raft trip down a big, uncharted river."

Suddenly, I saw the relevance of all the rivers and streams I had played in as a kid. I could talk river with this Voice. Pondering the similarities between the inner and outer rivers was the foundation of our conversation.

It was a relief to have someone to talk to. The Voice had come to my rescue in much the same way Wayne Elmore did when we were ten and eleven years old, exploring the woods the afternoon they were on fire. We got separated, and I was alone with nothing but smoke and fire all around. Ten years old and frantic, I was just about to lose it and cry when Wayne came running in through the smoke to find me and show me a way out. Relief poured through me. The Voice and Wayne had been aware that I was in deep trouble when they made their presence known.

The words and sound of the Moody Blues formed clear images in my mind that I began to see and understand. They sang, "Just open your mind (heart and eyes) and you will find the way it's always been." I realized that a new world of consciousness existed, one that had always been there, and yet no one had ever spoken a word about it. That realization resulted in an unbelievable high that built and intensified as the music continued, eventually climaxing as I heard the words from "Threshold of a Dream:" Now, you know that you are real.

Yes, it makes sense to love everyone and to make everyone your friend. Yes, there is a purpose in understanding deeper levels beyond our cultural education and lifestyle. I could see a higher purpose to life, and I noticed that others were talking about it in a clear and yet almost sneaky way through the medium of late Sixties' and early Seventies' rock and roll.

The reason I was alive started to make sense. The image of the river could be both internal and external, depending on my perspective. The river could be brown and muddy, stagnant, or crystal-clear and flowing. How it was depended on the thoughts and feelings moving through my consciousness. I felt as though I had driven my car into a car wash, windows completely covered with mud, and had come out the other end to see the light of day for the first time. The difference in clarity astounded me. Imagine if the muddy, polluted Passaic River suddenly became crystal-clear and drinkable.

This reminds me of my mother when she woke up in the hospital one morning during the winter of 1980. She had been completely out of it for several weeks after taking the wrong combination of prescription drugs and alcohol for too many days in a row. I thought for sure that she would die, and then— surprise—one morning she woke up completely clear-headed and asked, "What am I doing in the hospital?" Her body and mind had finally detoxed; the muddy river that had flowed through her consciousness had cleared, like a jet plane rising above the fog after take-off. It takes focus and energy to stay above the fog.

My life changed quickly after my experience in Florida. The influence of the cleaner, clearer river water was undeniable. It was now a few weeks before my twentieth birthday, and for the first time, I was holding on to some form of undeniable truth within me. I was no longer assuming that others had more awareness than I. It changed the direction of my life to see and feel the inner river. There was no going back. I knew that. I was determined to find out what this new awareness had to offer; it was the only thing I was interested in. What others thought about my interest didn't matter unless they could tell me about the river.

Chapter 3:
THE ARMY

My military draft notice came in the mail.

On the night before I was inducted into the army, I cut my long hair in front of the mirror I had looked into for my entire life. I went down to my room in the basement, got stoned, and listened to the Moody Blues. I trusted the river of my consciousness, which had become the flow of my life, both internally and externally.

In the morning, Dad dropped me off at the army induction building, which just happened to be in downtown Paterson. As soon as I got out of the car, I could see and feel an unknown river canyon pulling me forward, so I did my best to situate myself in the middle of my inner current before entering.

Along with ten other boys who had pulled low draft numbers, I took "The Oath" to serve in the military. From there, we were loaded into a bus and shipped to Fort Dix, located a few hours south in the central flatlands of the New Jersey Pine Barrens. Upon arrival, we were directed to a bunkhouse with fifty beds, which would be our home for our first two nights. In that bunkhouse, the Paterson-area boys merged with boys from as far away as Maine and Kentucky. Once all fifty of our new platoon had arrived, we were marched through a series of gates like cattle being moved for branding. At the first gate, they cut off all our hair. It was a major funny show to watch the looks on people's faces when their long hair and big afros dropped to the floor.

With our GI haircuts, we were marched over to the supply house, where we stood in line to get our army greens and boots. That is where I first met Kaddue. I was pretty sure he came directly from mommy and a family of mommy girls. He was short, innocent looking, and soft. When it was his turn, the supply sergeant asked, "What size shorts?"

"I don't know," he said. "My mother always bought my shorts." It was precious.

We were marched back to the bunkhouse to change into army greens. Everyone headed off to the bathroom to have a look in the mirror. It was a bit of a shock for us to see our shaven heads, but the black boys who had lost their huge afros saw the biggest change. Afros in those days stuck out three to eight inches, which gave a five-foot-six-inch guy the illusion that he was close to six feet tall. In 1972, cutting our hair and making us all dress in army greens was the simplest way to get fifty boys from all walks of life to shed a good part of their visual identity.

As a group, we were consciously simplified by the authorities. The long history of humanity's recruiting and training of boys to be soldiers was mastered long ago. Thus, once we agreed to the oath "to serve and protect," the playing field we had known all our lives was leveled to the bare basics. Each individual called upon his raw mental, emotional, and physical abilities to survive. Momma, big brother, schoolmates, and close friends were replaced by a group of strangers, all following orders from some drill sergeant who had all the power.

All of us were dumped into the river at the mouth of Army Canyon at the same time. We came with nothing but the clothes on our backs and maybe a few dollars in our wallets. We were provided everything we needed. The army clothed, fed, and sheltered us; they attended to us medically and controlled our movements. They gave us a duffel bag so we could carry everything we owned in one move.

By the evening of the second night, we had been stripped down and were prepared to start training on the following day. After dinner on that longest day of the year, the summer solstice, the drill sergeants left us alone. This was our first opportunity to talk among ourselves. Where are you from? What's your name? Did you get drafted or enlist, etc. The first in-depth conversation I remember had to do with the physical training we were about to go through. The question came up, "How many pushups can you do?" People hit the floor and banked up as many as they could, maybe twenty or thirty. Kaddue, the momma's boy, was looking on when I asked, "How many can you do?" He didn't know. He said he had never tried to do a push-up. I said, "Okay, man, this is serious. We are about to go through boot camp, and you can't do one push-up? Let's see what you got!"

And no, he couldn't do even one push-up! Oh, man! I could hardly comprehend it. But everyone had compassion for Kaddue. We couldn't bring ourselves to pick on the kid, and even the drill sergeants cut him some slack. When it came to physical fitness, he was the obvious runt with a good attitude. It served no purpose to pick on the weakling. Later, he became an inspiration in our training.

How did we know to have compassion for Kaddue instead of picking on him? In the animal world, he would have been eaten alive long before reaching physical maturity. Kaddue, I reckoned, was like a little brother who needed protection. It came naturally to our platoon, but that is not always the case, as some people are like wild animals tearing into the weak.

The third morning in the bunkhouse, we were told to pack our duffel bags. It was time to move into our new barracks. Initially, the order to "fall in" had produced confusion and fumbling. Now we responded instantly and immediately, leaving the bunkhouse at double-time and making it outside to the fall-in area without questioning or confusion and ready to march off to a new place. By that third morning, it took our fifty-man platoon less than five minutes to move into formation with ease. The sergeants noticed which privates were continually late, and five rows of ten men all lined up makes that easy. Within forty-eight hours of taking the oath, we had been converted into a group body and marched over to our new barracks, where we filled the second floor of a building perfectly built to house fifty men. Below us on the first floor was another platoon, and across the way from our building was a mirror-image that housed the third and fourth platoons of our Company B.

With our duffel bags over our shoulders, we walked up the stairs and entered what would be our home for the next ten weeks. There were rooms on the left and right, each with eight beds. We were to enter a room and grab our bunk and locker. This is how we filled up the barracks.

Your bed and your neighbor were the luck of the draw. I dropped my bag on the open bed next to the window in what turned out to be a room full of good guys. But for everyone at this particular moment, it was time to claim our space and let the experience unfold.

A little sidebar history lesson: By June 20, 1972, the army draft was in its last months of actively calling men for the war. All totaled, the effort for the war drafted one million, eight hundred thousand boys between 1963 and 1972. In 1968, around the time Dennis was drafted, the military was drafting 40,000 men a month! In my estimation, by the time I got drafted, at least one million, seven hundred seventy five thousand young men had gone before me.

In some ways, I imagine getting drafted is like going away to college and living in a freshman dorm. At its core, it is the experience of leaving the nest for the first time, an event that forces us to become independent. We are alone, that is, until we find our first new, real friend, and in time a circle of friends—except we were in the army and were going through the early stages of having our individuality broken down.

We were lined up for inoculations. Bam! in the left arm, then bam! in the right with some kind of needleless gun that forced the drugs through the skin and didn't need sterilization between shots. How many inoculations all at once? I have no idea, but after that, they let us go back to our barracks for the remainder of the day. The shots that hurt going in stopped hurting after the shot itself, but the easy, painless shots came on strong with pain the following day.

If you had eyes, it was easy to see the troublemakers well in advance. The big boulders in the middle of the river are easy to avoid. They were the wild boys that couldn't deal with restrictions or following orders.

I met more than a few guys that entered the army voluntarily because the judge gave them the option of jail or the military. Many of these guys were already starting out on the wrong foot and had no desire to be told to change their ways. It could be as simple as not waking up when the drill sergeant walked down the hall at three-thirty a.m., banging on a metal garbage can and yelling, "Get the fuck up!" These wild boys would leap out of their skins like wild cats that had just been caged! No one dared to get within reach. But the drill sergeants did. These boys were made examples.

Together as a fifty-man platoon, we learned to march in step when the sergeant yelled, "Give me your left!"

The platoon yelled back in unison, "You got it!" while slamming down the left foot.

"Give me your right!"

"You got it!" We slammed down the right foot.

Eventually, we were able to march while singing songs. Calvin, our platoon leader, was a black guy with a round, happy face and a strong singing voice. Halfway through boot camp, our platoon theme song became, "Lean on Me." I didn't know this Bill Withers song until Calvin started up, and eventually we all sang loud and clear.

This is one of the best songs in the world to bring about group unity. Sing, "I'll be your friend, I'll help you carry on," and soon everyone begins to feel it. The bad apples were sweetening up, and Kaddue started getting in shape for the first time in his life.

It was a group high, and I was high, getting totally fit, and enjoying a relatively peaceful stretch of the river that didn't require much thinking. To a practical guy like me, it made no sense to get the attention of the drill sergeant. Almost always, I fell into group formation somewhere in the middle rows. I had no desire to be a leader and no desire to stand out.

• • •

One hot, muggy afternoon in July, the drill sergeant told us we could go up to our rooms for a rest. How sweet was that? I quickly grabbed my towel from my locker and jumped into the deliciously cold shower. I was in heaven for about thirty seconds when I heard the famous, loud words ring through the halls of our barracks: "Fall in!'

"Shit!" I thought. Those motherfuckers are just busting our balls!" I charged out of the shower and down the hall. While cornering to enter my room, my wet feet slid, catching my left baby toe on the edge of the door jamb and ripping it back nearly to the side of my foot. The skin and muscle between the two toes tore, and it fucking hurt. I had to go to the infirmary for stitches. For obvious reasons, I no longer could march the five miles to and from the training ground in the sometimes over 90-degree weather at 90-percent humidity. So sad.

Since I had been given a medical excuse, I hitched rides in the water truck, food truck, or any other truck that was going to the training grounds. When the time had arrived that my foot had healed enough to resume marching, no one was keeping track, so I kept taking it easy. Then, one Friday night, the drill sergeant set us free to go on weekend leave. I took off for the barracks, running at full blast. I was busted. Come Monday morning, the sergeant made it clear that I would be marching, and all the drill sergeants had learned my name. Surprisingly, they never gave me a hard time for jumping in the shower or for finding out I had been milking my injury.

Our platoon had somehow developed the magical ability to energetically tie together all of our individual rafts into one large, group raft. In other words, we dropped our personal concerns in order to benefit the unit. Simply by the luck of the draw, we, the first platoon of the four-platoon Company B, had a harmonious platoon compared to the other three. Our platoon was filled mostly with draftees and/or guys with common sense, which made a big difference. Some came from very simple rural areas, while others came from the heart of a ghetto. Most of us graduated from high school but didn't go on to college.

Having accepted my fate well before entering Basic Training, I subconsciously held on to two beliefs: one, that the experience of entering the army would "teach me something," and two, that if I needed to, I could get out. These unquestioned assumptions had been planted sometime during or shortly after the Florida Moody Blues trip.

Backed by those comforting thoughts I made the choice to go with the flow. Now, it was time to adjust to the new environment and trust in my ability to learn new survival skills, both internally and externally.

The inner and the outer rivers of my life became more or less the same. This happens when you are able to be totally in the moment. The water moves so fast that there is no time to think about what might happen tomorrow. I needed to pay attention to what was happening in this moment, of this hour, of this day. No thinking about what might happen after Basic Training or around the next bend in the canyon unless you wanted to get tossed overboard to learn that, indeed, the river is very cold and overpowering to a man without a boat or life jacket.

Out at the shooting range during our first introduction to the M16, the drill sergeant stood in front of us, facing the targets. He fired at the targets by placing the stock of the weapon against his balls and pulling the trigger. Perhaps ten rounds went off, and he did wince once. We were all shocked, yet at the same time, we laughed. M16s with their big bullets have no kick!

This was going to be fun! Always as a kid I had enjoyed shooting or throwing things into the air: small, round rocks in a sling shot; spears made from tiny tree saplings; smooth rocks; bows and arrows; water pistols; or the toys guns that could shoot spring-loaded plastic bullets.

Often in good weather, we boys had played make-believe war against the Germans or Cowboys and Indians with our toy guns. While outside in the winter, we had snowball fights among friends. While inside, we were constantly exposed to the war on the evening news and in gun-battle television Westerns. However, it should be pointed out that the emotional waves of sorrow and pain and the spectacle of death associated with the blood and guts of actual war were 100 percent censored both on television and during our Army Basic Training. My only experience with actually feeling the violence caused by a gun had occurred when I accidently killed some baby birds in a nest with a BB gun. That action had resulted in perhaps my first experience of feeling the wave of sadness.

So, yes, pulling the trigger and hitting targets in Basic Training was designed to be fun for kids like me. Yet, in all ten weeks of Basic

Training, we were given zero preparation for the mental and emotional trauma of killing. It was simply never added to the mix.

One day after we had been trained to fire M16s, we were guided down into a concrete bunker that had a metal roof. One by one, we stepped out of the shelter and into a grenade-tossing chamber. While the drill sergeant stood next to and guided each private, we pulled the pin and threw the grenade as far as we could. When it was my turn, I tossed the grenade with all my might out into the open field. From the protected observation tower above, another drill sergeant spoke through the loud speaker. "Excellent. That was the farthest toss of the day!" It sure made me feel good. We heard fifty grenades detonating and pouring metal rain upon our protective roof that day.

What was I thinking? Was I even thinking at all? I know now that the twenty-year-old personality was treating this army stuff as a sporting event or a competition of some sort.

I had always thrived on healthy competition among the boys in our community. Baseball, football, and basketball were the Little League sports we all enjoyed. Among a small group of close friends, we measured: Who caught the biggest fish? Who climbed the highest on a particular tree? Who could skim a rock the furthest across the river? Always we had fun being boys.

So, I was not surprised to have the furthest grenade toss. Shit. I probably had tossed more rocks, spears, baseballs, and footballs than 99 percent of the kids my age in the whole country. But for the life of me, I never once thought that the drill sergeants might be taking notes on which of us would be the best private to toss the grenade into enemy camp.

Every day as a platoon, we marched somewhere, as most of the training grounds were a good five miles away. The roads were dirt, really dry dirt, during the summer of 1972. My memory banks remind me that there was no rain that summer.

When all four platoons marched as a company in the heat of that New Jersey summer, our platoon always led the way to and from the training grounds. We didn't know why we always went first until near the end of training when the drill sergeants decided that our platoon would march last. Holy shit! For the whole time, the other guys had been eating dust while a hundred fifty men ahead of them pounded their feet into the dirt road. We were shocked at how bad it was. That's when we discovered that the company's four-platoon drill sergeants had been running a competitive game. Each morning while the four platoons fell in for the morning head count and breakfast, the drill sergeants inspected all the platoon's barracks. How neat did you leave your bed? How clean were the rooms, the halls, the floors, and the bathrooms? Apparently, they had a grading system, and the winning platoon always got to lead the company.

By now, our platoon understood that we had a bond, so we had little trouble among our fifty boys. The three other platoons that made up our company were completely dysfunctional compared to ours. Our platoon had three or four of those big-boulder troublemakers, while each of the other platoons had ten or more. Those boulders were the Red Meat to satisfy all the drill sergeants' hunger. Our platoon's sergeant had it easy, because we dealt with our troublemakers like big brothers who help younger brothers. This allowed our drill sergeant to go home to his wife at night, knowing that his platoon was taking care of business. Always we got more sleep and breathed in less dust (except for that one day).

• • •

As a white boy with little or no experience with black kids, I learned a lot about blacks and their wide range of experience compared to mine. It was a black man who told me that there were both white and black niggers, which seemed to me just another name for an asshole. Being an asshole or a nigger had nothing to do with the color of your skin. I heard stories from boys deep in the ghetto who started cutting school when they were ten years old to get drunk in the alleys. I heard stories in which they sexually abused girls their own age, but not with sexual penetration, because the boys themselves were still too young to feel the sexual energy in their penises. Instead, they would piss in the girl's mouth. Other boys already had bullet wounds and decided to join the army because they thought it would be safer.

There were other stories from the country boys who grew up in rural areas so isolated that walking to a friend's house after school or in the summer was not an option. Fishing and playing in Mother Nature were things I could relate to with these guys. They told stories of family tomato fights out in the late-summer garden, in which Mom, Dad, and all the siblings were involved. I imagine Wayne's dad came from a place like that.

We had 516 kids in our 1970 graduation class, while these guys had maybe ten. Some of the guys were simple-minded when it came to interactions among people. Although they had grown up in the 1950s and 60s like all of us, the culture of rock and roll and weed had not yet reached their home towns. Were they perhaps the 10 or 15 percent of Americans who didn't have a television during those years?

For the most part, I listened with no judgment. Since we had all been cut down to the raw bone, we all had the opportunity to start anew.

We were a mixed bag of black and white boys, and for most of us, this was our first experience of interacting daily with guys of a different color. That turned out to be a huge blessing for all as we began to trust and watch out for each other's back. As we marched and sang our songs, our individual rafts were woven together by the energetic thread of brotherhood.

I remember a guy named Julian Baxter. He was from Harlem and was early "Red Meat" for the sergeants. Baxter thought Carroll was a pussy's name. All he wanted to do was fight, not even caring if he won or lost. One day, he wanted to fight me, but I didn't take the bait. Many weeks later, on a Sunday afternoon near the end of Basic Training when I had returned from weekend leave, I entered the barracks. Even with no air conditioning and the windows wide open, I smelled weed. I got up and walked down the hall to the next room, and there was Baxter, blowing the smoke of his joint out the window. We laughed and smoked the rest of the joint together. Then he looked at me and said, "You know what? I don't like to fight! I realized it when I went home this weekend." Fighting had been just a way of life for him when he was growing up in the inner city, and here he was in the army, realizing he didn't want to fight anymore. How ironic. It felt good, and we were close for a few moments in time.

After that, I stayed focused on my training. Before bed every night, I did fifty sit-ups as fast as I could, and then I dropped down to the floor and did at least fifty push-ups on my fingertips. I was pumped and wanting to score high on the physical fitness test at the end of training.

• • •

One day during the final week of Basic Training, we marched to the physical-fitness test ground for our competition. I scored a perfect score in all but one event, until the final mile run, that is. During the sit-up competition, we had needed to do fifty in two minutes. I only did forty-nine. As we lined up for the beginning of the mile run, the sergeant told me he would give me the fifty sit-ups and a perfect score if I got a perfect score on the mile run. It was to be a six-minute mile run in army boots. We took off. I was alone out in front of the others when I finished in six minutes and one second.

The next few days passed like the last few days of school before the start of summer break. Our training was almost complete. It was late in the afternoon on the last day before we graduated and received our advanced training orders. You would think it was time for a celebration. But no, the sergeants decided to make us clean our rifles. Yes, we had cleaned the weapons many times before, but never like this. The drill sergeant sat at a table and inspected the weapon with a Q-tip-size white rag that could be pushed in the smallest of places. Any spec of darkness on the cloth was cause for rejection. We soon learned they had planned this unreasonable inspection to bust our balls. It dragged on for so long that many of us took it as a slap in the face after working our asses for ten weeks.

Eventually, my closest roommate gave up and started to express his feelings. First, he was pissed that he had volunteered to join the army with his best friend on the so-called "join the army buddy system," only to get separated as if the agreement had never been made. Second, he was so skinny and underweight that at the first attempt he failed the army physical. So, what did he do? He left the army induction building, went across the street to the local bank, and purchased a bunch of quarter rolls which he tied under his pant legs for the extra weight. Then he went back to the army physical building and passed the test.

After the way he had been treated in the last week of training, he felt a fool. Then he changed his focus to the weapon he held in his hand. He tossed it on his bed and said, "Look at it!" He began to speak of its true, cold ugliness of purpose. He was sickened.

During the entire ten weeks, never do I remember another such heavy talk.

The shadow hung over us that last night. It was the first night that we had to take the weapon to bed. It had been impressed upon us over and over the importance of being responsible for the weapon. You took it everywhere with you for fear that a drill sergeant might find it unattended. My friend locked his weapon in his locker and went to bed. Did I lock my weapon in the locker, or did I sleep with it in my arms? I can't remember.

In the morning before breakfast, everyone who still had a weapon was required to return it to the gunroom before fall-in head count and breakfast. Nothing more was said. Later in the morning, our Bravo Company of two hundred men would gather in the grandstands in front of our families and friends.

During the awards ceremony, my name was called to receive the Physical Fitness Award for my platoon. Out of the two hundred men, only one guy from another platoon had a better score. He had managed to do the fifty sit-ups as well as the mile run in under six minutes. I had just missed first place and a perfect score by one sit-up and one second. Not bad, I must say. I was once again in my glory as an athlete.

After graduation, we were given the afternoon off to visit with our guests. I was lucky to have Mom, Dad, and my girlfriend, Carolyn, as my guests, since many soldiers were alone.

Mom and Dad didn't stay long so they could make the drive back to West Paterson before the afternoon rush hour traffic broke loose. Carolyn had her own ride, so we decided to walk towards the woods where the other guys were heading with their girlfriends or to just go off and smoke a joint.

The afternoon passed in a flash, and before I knew it, I was kissing Carolyn good-bye at her car. It was time for the platoons to gather back at the barracks and receive our orders.

Up until that moment, I had never considered what would happen after Basic Training. No one other than my brother Dennis had spoken to me about the realities of the army. Dennis tried to shine an advance light on how the training process is designed to strip away our individualism so that one sergeant can yell, "Hit the prone!" (Hit the dirt with your body as flat as a pancake instantly and without thought) and a second later, see fifty men lying flat on the Earth. It's a good thing to know if a bomb is about to go off: Hit the prone!

I had never seriously considered what my advanced training might be. My goal early on in training was to get through it, do well on the fitness test, and see what happened. As we were waiting around for our advanced training orders, one of the sergeants spoke to me about my award in a very uplifting manor until he realized that our headmaster drill sergeant had forgotten to recommend me for a promotion from private to private first class (from no bar on the collar to one bar on the collar). He directly told me that he had never seen a private win his platoon's physical fitness award and not receive a promotion. Never! A few moments later, my name was called, and I received my Orders.

They read: INFANTRY TRAINING, Fort Jackson, South Carolina.

Realizing what infantry training meant immediately caused the banks of my inner river to contract. The water ran faster. I was very upset! This was not in my plan, or more correctly speaking, I was blind-sided because I never had a plan. What had I been thinking? Obviously, I wasn't thinking. Shit. Was this what the guy from Canada was trying to make me see? No one ever took me aside and spoke to me directly about how the army decides which "advanced training" to put the draftees through.

I was shaken to the core. Now, but not then, I flash to the tests we took on the afternoons when it was simply too hot to do physical work. They were the simplest tests I had ever taken. They asked simple questions like:

Choose from A or B: What would you rather do—A: Go to the

library, or B: Play baseball?

What would you rather do—A: Read a book, or B: Go fishing?

Of course, now it all makes sense. But at the time, I enjoyed taking a test that was easy to read and understand. Because of the dyslexia, school tests had never been that easy. For some reason, I didn't realize at the time that these army tests were the dividers. Those who chose A answers went to the office. Those who chose B answers went to the trenches. Dennis went to the office, and I went to the infantry. Never had I contemplated how the longest grenade toss, the physical fitness award, or the answers on my tests would determine where the army decided I should go for advanced training.

The group raft I had been attached to disappeared, and the Voice returned: "You got to get out of here!"

Into the Unknown

Chapter 4:
CONSCIENTIOUS OBJECTION

I could feel the current within me speeding up as it did when our 55-gallon-drum raft was nearly swept into the Passaic River. There was no controlling my raft. Mere hours after receiving the orders for infantry training, I was on the army bus heading south through the night to Fort Jackson, South Carolina.

By mid-morning I was lined up in formation with fifty soldiers from other military bases around the country. This was our new advanced infantry platoon. The drill sergeant, a big man with a shaved head, addressed his new platoon with a question: "All right, men, who wants McGovern for president?" (McGovern ran against Nixon for president in November 1972.) I was the only one who raised his hand. Now, to be honest, my awareness of presidential politics at the time was near zero. I raised my hand for McGovern only because Walter Who's sister, who had invited us to Canada, also worked for the NYC McGovern for President campaign. Through her connection, Walter and I got free tickets to the George McGovern presidential rally at Madison Square Garden. Yes, we had great seats and we heard McGovern speak. But the only reason we were there was to hear the after-speech concert performances by Peter, Paul and Mary and Simon and Garfunkel.

Back in formation with fifty new guys and without much thinking or reflection on my Basic Training philosophy of "Do not attract the attention of the drill sergeant." I slipped, and in less than five minutes, Private Carroll took the first easy bait tossed out by the drill sergeant. It was obvious that the sergeant liked Nixon, who was still his commander and chief.

This first assembly of the platoon took place in the late morning on the last day before the start of Labor Day weekend. It was great luck that, after this quick, official gathering, we were set free for the long weekend.

One of the guys and I decided to hitchhike the hundred and fifty miles east to Myrtle Beach for the weekend. We left late that afternoon traveled through the night. We got rides the whole way from mostly local, wild boys who were drinking and cruising the highway for entertainment.

This Labor Day weekend, the river had mellowed out enough that I could actually enjoy some time in relative peace after a crazy ride that started the moment I stepped out of my dad's car at the base. I spent the next few days walking the wave line between the ocean and the beach while reconnecting with my inner voice, which was yelling, "You've got to get out of here!

Resuming the inner dialogue I had begun during Spring Break five months earlier in Florida was a process of reorientation something like coming back to consciousness after being knocked out or reestablishing a relationship after being away. It was a time to catch-up and get reacquainted. The skill of listening to my inner guide was in its infancy, yet it was coming in loudly enough that I did not doubt its authenticity. It had a certain reality and clarity in my thoughts and feelings. I didn't know it at the time, but this was the voice of my higher self/soul aspect, talking to its little brother self, whose mission it was to wake up.

Today, I see it as my true Self communicating with my personality self, which was confused by, and in dramatic conflict with, the cultural norms I was caught up in.

At that time, there was no other person I could talk to about my dilemma. The head doctor I would see in another month or two would be the first to recognize that something different was going on in me: I was determined to do something to break out of the current belief system, which was trying to train me to kill.

By the grace of the Labor Day holiday, I had a few days to contemplate my situation and realign my raft once again to the center of the river. There were no clear answers or pathways to my future other than knowing that infantry training was waiting around the next, rapidly approaching bend. I was in a state of consciousness called "high alert."

My buddy and I managed to get back to our barracks in time for a shower and some sleep before the first early morning fall-out call rang through the barracks' hallway.

All two hundred men that formed the new infantry company were recent graduates of Basic Training from different military bases around the country. We were all in top physical condition. Psychologically, we were all over the place, and it was clear from the beginning that everybody hadn't had the brotherly experience I'd had during basic. Tangible energetic friction ran beneath between black/white and Spanish/Mexican boys. I stood clear of it, as I had no bones to pick and felt physically confident to hold my own.

One day, I happened to be standing next to the mess hall sergeant when two black guys started fighting. The sergeant looked at me and said, "They are fighting over a hole, shit, and if they want a hole, I can get them a hole."

The point here is that once we graduated from Basic to Advanced Training, privates no longer had KP duty. The military instead hired a civilian staff to do that job. These were mostly, if not all, black girls from the surrounding area. Apparently, some of these civilian woman workers were willing to work as prostitutes for the sergeant's side business. At a basic level, this guy viewed females as holes for a man's release and pleasure and his profit. He was simply flabbergasted that two guys would waste their time fighting over a "hole." Once again, my eyes and ears were exposed to new and different realities from the population of our country.

To clarify, in Basic Training, everyone within the two-hundred man company pulled at least one kitchen duty (KP) day during the cycle of training. One day, my name and a few others were called out of our platoon for KP duty. This happened while we were out in the field, preparing to spend our one night camping in the woods in our pup tents. Because we KP boys had to report to mess hall at four a.m. the next morning for duty, we were told that we would have to go back and sleep in the barracks for the night. We were lucky. It was a very hot, humid, New Jersey summer night. I remember it well. That evening, I sat on the cool shower floor under the cold spray for more than an hour before I'd had enough. It was one of the best evenings and nights of Basic Training, being alone in the fifty-man barracks with only three or four other guys. We were fortunate to avoid the platoon pup-tent experience.

KP itself was not hard. Mostly I remember myself and two other guys cracking hundreds of eggs into a big pot to be scrambled later by the cook. Every once in a while, we'd see a bloody baby chicken in its early stages of development drop into the pot! We did nothing but laugh and avoided the scrambled eggs in the future. Of course, there were mice in the kitchen, but in general, everything was kept clean.

Within the first few days of training, we were all required to sit behind a 50-caliber machine gun, aim at targets several hundred feet out in the firing range, pull the trigger, and try to blast holes in human-shaped targets.

Unexpected and unseen, like the first rumblings of an impending earthquake, my body began to shake. When I was able to stand up again, I asked to go to the latrine. With permission, I started walking down the dirt path to the outdoor piss latrine (which happened to be a large, galvanized-metal watering bucket that one might expect to see on a cattle or horse farm, when I heard "Double time, Carroll, double time!" Hearing the words "double time" instantly triggered my trained response from Basic to quicken my pace. But my faster pace lasted only a few seconds before I returned to a walk. By the time I returned, the landscape had changed. It had become clear to me that my conversation with my inner voice had no intention of fading into the background as it had during Basic Training. It was now a part of a constant internal conversation.

Drill sergeants don't like it when a private in training disregards an order. Clearly, I was being eyed as "red meat." I had a contrary attitude that was starting to give the drill sergeant a case of the ass.

Our platoon drill sergeant's job was to make sure we got to the training grounds at the correct time every day, yet, it was not necessarily his job to train us in everything we learned. We had many weapons training' drill sergeants to help with that aspect of our education and, fortunately, none of them knew I had been marked as "Red Meat."

So, during target practice, I missed the human-silhouette targets on purpose. It drove the drill sergeants who didn't know me crazy. They'd grab my M16 and fire at the target to make sure the sight was adjusted correctly. When they gave it back to me, I'd aim just enough to the right or left to miss the target. They had no idea I was missing the target on purpose. When we trained with the 45-caliber handgun, we were also instructed on how to take the handgun apart, clean it, and put it back together. Somehow, I just couldn't figure out how to put the 45 back together. It didn't matter. There were no tests. And being a bad shot didn't mean they wouldn't send you off to some military conflict somewhere around the world.

Some days later, it was recommended that I visit the post chaplain, which I was happy to oblige. He welcomed me into his office with the warm friendliness you would expect from a priest/minister. It felt that he was taken, to some degree, by the passion I expressed in my story. I told it all the best I could, including the tripping on mescaline, and the return of the inner Voice that rejected the idea of being trained to kill. It was a wonderful conversation, as I remember, until he realized I had zero interest in attending Sunday church services or accepting Jesus as my personal savior. Only then, and by the grace of the river spirits, did he encourage me to become a conscientious objector.

For the first time, I had a course of action to take. I declared, "I am a Conscientious Objector (CO)," and was immediately taken out of training and told I had two weeks to handwrite a paper explaining my beliefs.

With no dictionary, twenty Ds, and four Fs in high-school English, I started to look inside my head for something to write down on paper as a presentation to the army about my strongly felt feelings and beliefs. The obvious place to look was within the Catholic religion. Surely there might be something there. But no, I could find nothing in my memory banks to back up my feelings. Never do I remember hearing a Catholic nun or priest speak out against war. Yes, killing another human was a mortal sin in the Catholic religion, but for some reason, killing the enemy in war didn't enter into the teachings.

For the most part, I had remained sound asleep when it came to paying attention to the drama playing out on the world stage. Sure, I was aware of the anti-war movement. But it was in the same way I was aware of Woodstock. It had not penetrated into my awakened feeling consciousness until then. In other words, my education didn't tell me I should resist being trained to kill other humans. It was a struggle to find the words to express my feelings as the deadline for the paper neared. At the last moment, I decided to write about the mescaline trip I had taken during Spring Break. Life was for living, loving, and bringing peace to the world! Signed, Private Carroll.

A few weeks later, I received the order to report to the captain in charge of reviewing the Conscientious Objectors' Papers.

Before he told me the decision on my paper, he asked about my drug use. I assured him that, yes, as told in the story I did take drugs, but no longer found them enjoyable.

After that, he proceeded to tell me a gruesome story he had witnessed in Vietnam. While on patrol, they found the bodies of several American soldiers. They had been staked out naked under the flowing river with their genitals cut off and stuffed into their mouths. Then, he looked me straight in the eye and asked if that was what I objected to. I said, "Yes, Sir!"

His report stated that Private Carroll was not sincere in his beliefs and therefore should not be let out of the Army.

Nonetheless, by still claiming CO status, I was granted the legal right not to be trained to kill. Years earlier, I am sure, during the heat of the war, I would have been put directly into a medic unit or some other job that didn't require carrying a gun and shipped off to Vietnam, anyway, or perhaps sent directly to jail if I still refused. Now, however, in the fall of 1972, the war was winding down, draftees no longer went to Vietnam, and it appeared that they didn't need or have a place to put the troublemakers like me.

I was assigned to maintenance detail with a few other guys who were in similar situations. I raked leaves, picked up trash, and, on occasion, was assigned as a part-time driver for the local major.

Something had shifted. By taking the chaplain's advice, I learned that I could indeed alter the direction of my raft inside these canyon walls. For the moment, I was taking a breather, my job like camping out to rest on a small patch of beach along the river.

During this period, I began to get the impression that the army was, or would be, willing to offer me a different area of advanced training. Never did they provide a list of choices, but I do remember them hinting at the possibility, perhaps just to see if I would once again take the bait. However, it was too late. I had seen and heard enough to become completely soured on the idea of staying in the army, and I wanted out. Perhaps, if it had unfolded differently for me, as it did with one of my Basic Training friends who had grown up in a family that owned an electrical company. He was already a trained electrician, and for him, there was no Advanced Training. Instead, he went directly from Boot Camp to the electrical/construction unit at Fort Jackson. If they had offered me training as a construction worker, I would have jumped at the opportunity. But I'd had no such training.

After several weeks of "rest," a new feeling of restlessness started to brew as I came face to face with the reality that I wasn't going anywhere, and that I would likely continue to rake leaves and pick up trash at the lowest army rank for another twenty months. I felt like a restless racehorse that needed to get out of the barn and run. After many long conversations with The Voice, I pushed my raft back into the river. I decided to continue training, hoping to find another way out.

The officers were happy to hear that I had decided to see the light. They quickly assigned me to a new company commander and platoon, where I would continue my training where I left off when I became The Objector.

On the first day, we were marched out to the woods to be trained in the art of ambushing the enemy. The training grounds at Fort Jackson were similar to those at Fort Dix in that both were in pine forests and featured plenty of space and many trees. This provided easy maneuvering through the trees on the pine-needle carpeted floor. Off to the right was the dusty dirt road that we had arrived on and upon which we had continued to meander through the woods. It was obvious that the "enemy" would be coming from that direction.

In preparation, we were given special green and black army-issue face paints and told to experiment. There was no mirror in which to check out our application, and we played like children. Then, we picked up branches and twigs from the underbrush and tucked them into our helmets or attached them to our army greens. "Okay," I thought, "I know this game!" I had played it hundreds of times in the woods with the neighborhood boys. The M16s we carried were filled with blanks. In other words, they were similar to the cap guns and toy rifles we boys had. Both the M16 and cap gun made the crack! sound when we pulled the trigger, and neither shot a projectile out of the barrel. No one was going to spill blood and guts on the pine needle carpet that day.

As a platoon, we were called back into formation to be given the final instructions before ambushing the enemy, who would at some point be coming down the road. We were told emphatically that we were to "make believe" this was "the real thing." We were told that there would be men, women, and children, and that we were to kill everyone. We were then told to find a hiding spot and wait for the order to open fire.

I was well hidden under a bush when the enemy approached and the drill sergeant gave the order, "Open fire!" We all started running around in the trees, shooting blanks at each other like we did in the woods back in West Paterson. Bang! You are dead! But no, he wasn't really dead; he simply ran to another tree and started firing off blanks again.

That was the breaking point. I'd had enough of this bullshit; we played better war games as kids back in the early Sixties with water pistols that were at times filled with piss! We kids also had water balloons to use as hand grenades, and everyone knew if they got hit, they had to fall to the ground like we saw on television. Then, we would get up and start all over again.

I was somewhat paralyzed under a bush when the drill sergeant noticed I had not yet fired my weapon. I simply could not aim my M16 at the boys from the 2nd platoon and make believe they were an enemy of men, women, and children to be killed. He yelled, "You're disobeying a direct order. Fire that weapon, Carroll! At that moment, a small fork in the river appeared off to my right, and yes, I could feel it pulling me in, and I saw the sign "Defiance Canyon."

Without a thought, as if it were as natural a response as regaining your balance when you trip or blocking your face when you get sprayed in the face, I rolled over and fired the weapon's clip full of blanks into the sky. In ferocious and immediate reaction, the sergeant went into a fit, his mouth drooling as if at the sight of, well, red meat! He puffed himself up like a boxer or a huge, mean wrestler and was about to kick my ass just as the second lieutenant made his presence known. Instantly, the playground bully transformed his anger from thoughts of an old-fashioned whooping into a verbal assault, instead. He hurled a long list of curses: "You motherfucker, shithead, bulkhead, piece of shit! It's people like you that get others killed in war!" With the second lieutenant standing close by, I replied, "I don't ever plan to get in that situation, Drill Sergeant."

It was all I could do. How could I aim a gun at those people and pull the trigger? This was the real thing or, at least, this was the closest thing to the real thing I had ever experienced. I could feel the heat. Perhaps I was being viewed by out-of-body souls of men who themselves had killed and been killed in war and wished they had made a different choice. I felt I was receiving outside encouragement from some source in another dimension. For sure, my inner-voice connection was present, to the extent that it could take over as the expert oarsman to save my boat from flipping.

Finally, it had hit home completely. The fun and games were completely over. Defiance Canyon separated my boat from all the others. The army trainer said to "make believe" this was the real thing, and it was clear to me now that I would not allow myself to be trained to kill.

That day, my action of shooting the M16 up in the air made a black man in my platoon mad at me. He just didn't like me, and he made it known to others that he wanted to fight. I was not afraid and told his friends as much. I was strong, and he would have to be a big motherfucker to kick my ass. The tension continued mounting over several days until one evening in the barracks. I got up from my bunk to go and get a soda from the machine. A friend stopped me at the top of the stairs, saying, "You better not go down there. They are waiting for you."

It just turned out to be one of those things you can't avoid. This narrow canyon was wide enough for only one boat. Any boulder in the way had to be faced and dealt with directly. There was no way around the situation. I made my way to the soda machine area.

The guy was there with several friends and a few onlookers. We stood face to face like two boxers, eyeing each other seconds before the bell. He was no bigger than I and perhaps slightly thinner.

Right away, he wanted to take this confrontation outside; and right away, I replied, "No way!" There was no rope or ring to contain the fight, but a circle of soldiers surrounded us. One eager soldier, wanting to see a fight, pushed me into my opponent to get it started.

The punches flew, and then two of his friends jumped in to help their friend. The fight didn't last long because I held my ground. When the punches stopped, we lowered our hands. The fight appeared to be over, and then one of his friends punched me in the mouth when I wasn't looking. That was the last punch, and the only punch to draw blood. That was it. The fight was over, and just like a male sexual orgasm, the tension and pressure dissipated. The three-on-one fight wasn't fair, but it wasn't until several weeks further downstream that I understood that.

At the time, I had a few friends who wanted to get even after they heard about the three-on-one pile-on. But I would have nothing to do with it. The tension was gone. I had never wanted to fight and only did so because I had been faced with an unavoidable section of the river that tested my courage. In return, I was granted a new level of respect among the boys in the platoon.

On another training, we had to wait until night. We had to practice escaping prison in the darkness and making our way through the dark forest without getting caught by the other platoon, which lay in wait somewhere between Point A, where we escaped, and Point B, where we had been instructed to go.

Early in the escape, my friend and I decided to run only a few hundred yards and then stop to rest against a tree and wait. We knew no one was chasing us from behind and that guys were trying to catch us if we moved forward. This made sense to us until the crack-blasts from blank grenades started going off around us. Holy fucking shit! The brass never figured that two privates would stop running away from prison, and the two of us had no idea they would be blowing these things up after the escape! Any closer and we would have lost our hearing, or worse. We ran our fucking asses off. By the time we made it through the forest to Point B, the game was over. Some made it and others got caught. There was no test, only a head count, and it was similar to the ambush training in that we only practiced one side of the experience. Great education? Ha!

Orienteering training happened one afternoon. Now, remember, this was before the invention of GPS systems. After being instructed on how to read a map and use a compass, our platoon broke up into groups of four. As in a treasure hunt, X marked the spots on the map that we were to find. As my group of four went our separate way, one of the guys pulled out a joint. We found a nice spot in the woods, fired it up, and passed it around until it was gone. After that, we did not look at the map or try to find the Xs. An hour or two later, the game was over; no test, only a head count. Afternoons like this were rare. These were the moments when human connections merged, and, if only for a brief moment, our rafts were tied together.

One afternoon I was called to the major's office for a talk about my attitude. As a reference point, there are four platoons to a company, and five companies, or a thousand men, to a battalion. The major was in charge of the battalion.

As I remember, he was a very nice guy who had probably encountered a few privates like me over the years. He looked me straight in the eye and said, "I know you want out of the army, but I can't let you out because you haven't done anything wrong." He referred to my record in Basic Training, where I had won the PT test, a sharp-shooter medal, and had been offered the opportunity to go to officer's training school. In other words, my recent acts of defiance and my application as a Conscientious Objector were the reasons for this conversation, and cause for concern, but were not serious enough to warrant discharge. I responded, "Then I'll have to do something wrong, Sir." He looked me in the eye and said, "I am betting that you won't."

When you're on the river, you do what is necessary to keep from drowning. After leaving his office, I went back to my bunk, opened my locker, packed my bag, and walked directly to the closest bus stop without hesitation. Within hours, or certainly by the next morning's Fall-out head count, I was legally considered AWOL. The act itself was similar to when I walked downstairs for the soda, willing to directly face the turbulent waters, in order to get a little further downstream. I handed the bus driver enough cash to get me to Myrtle Beach.

I felt at home when I got off the bus in Myrtle Beach. It was easy to find the friend I had met the year before, and he invited me to crash on his floor. He had been in the military and understood my situation.

Again, like I did over Labor Day, I spent most of the day walking up and down the beach, contemplating my situation with The Voice. The gentle ocean waves soothed my nerves. It was a much-needed break from the intense mental focus I had needed in order to avoid getting flipped out into the turbulent water that ran through Fort Jackson.

Long stretches of difficult Class 3 and 4 river conditions can be exhausting. Without proper rest, eventually the boat will get flipped. In this way, it was perfect timing that another little fork off to the side of the river appeared. It was similar to Defiance Canyon, and it was named Get Away Canyon. I had headed down that canyon the moment I walked out of the majors' office.

The major, in essence, had made a bet with me. Actually, it was more than "in essence." What he had put before me was a rock-solid bet. Little did he know that, in high school, I'd made gas money by playing poker on the weekends and pitching quarters on the school pavement. In pitching quarters, the rules are: Stand behind the line, toss the quarter to the wall; closest to the wall wins all the quarters. There were times when one good toss could rake in two bucks. I played almost every day with a few of my friends. We took money from classmates like a slot machine takes the last coin from a gambler's pocket. I had learned to play penny-nickel poker at my parents' dining room table when I was ten years old. The point here is, the Major made a bet with me, he bet me I wouldn't, and I took that bet when I replied, "Well, I guess I'll have to do something wrong."

After five or six days in the beautiful Myrtle Beach sun, it was time I hitchhiked back to the fort and faced the music. I had no clear path, but I did hope and dream that the major would let me out of the army as payment for losing the bet.

Upon my return, I went directly to my captain's office. "Private Carroll reporting back to duty, Sir!" I said, including the proper salute.

He was very calm and happy that I had returned and asked why I had gone AWOL. I explained that I needed to get away and think about my situation. Again in a calm and clear tone, he said that he understood my need to get away, and then he gave me an Article 218, which is the equivalent of an expensive speeding ticket, and ordered me to return to training.

It became obvious that going AWOL once was not getting me discharged from the army. Each morning, our platoon fell into formation for a head count and a showing of hands for those needing sick call. I raised my hand every day. I needed help, and eventually discovered that a social worker was available to listen to my problem. He was a smart guy with a college education. He had been drafted, like me, and was doing his time. It some ways, he reminded me of my brother Dennis, not fit for fighting, but with a good office and communication skills. He heard my story and made an appointment for me to see the psychiatrist.

A few days later, I was in the doctor's office, telling my story, when he asked, "Why do you want out of the army, Private Carroll?"

"I don't want to be trained to kill," I said, "There is a pressure in my head and a feeling I have, but I can't put it into words."

"What do you want to do with your life?"

I told him, "I want to do something fun, like be a scuba diver." Honestly, I didn't know what I wanted to do, but I always enjoyed Sea Hunt, starring Mike Nelson. Like Flipper, it had been a favorite.

As I left, the social worker gave me a wink and said I should be out in a week or two. I was overjoyed and returned to my platoon with the confidence that I would be discharged. Two weeks passed, and not a word came about my discharge. I raised my hand at morning sick call and went back to the social worker. He was a little surprised that there had been no movement toward my discharge and decided to go into the doctor's office and read what the psychiatrist had put on my report.

It said, "Private Carroll should be let out of the army if he refuses to train; otherwise he may act out in multiple ways." Simple enough, I thought. I would refuse to train. Confidently, I walked back to my captain's office and told him that I refused to train. What else was there for me to do? As with Defiance Canyon and Get Away Canyon, I had now entered Refuse to Train Canyon." Once inside this canyon, the captain directed my attention to two new canyons just up the way, Go to Jail or Go Back to Training canyons. Out of the kindness of the captain's heart, he gave me the morning to think about it.

What was there to think about? I had no intention of going to jail! Jail was for the bad guys, drug dealers, and thieves.

After lunch, I told the captain that I would go back to training to avoid going down Jail Canyon. Once again, in a mild manner, he said, "Yes, Private Carroll, you can go back to training. However, because you have missed too many days of training with your present platoon, you are now being transferred to a different company.

At the time, I was just grateful that my fate hadn't taken me over some waterfalls.

"Dismissed, Private Carroll."

"Yes, Sir!" I said. I saluted and walked out of the office. This was all taking place somewhere in 1972, some few days before Thanksgiving. The canyon walls were tightening as I walked through the maze of barracks and office buildings to my new company's headquarters.

I reported to my new captain with the proper salute and words: "Private Carroll reporting for duty, Sir." He was sitting at his desk, reviewing my paperwork, when he looked up and said, "Private Carroll, it says here that you are a Conscientious Objector."

"Yes, sir. I don't believe in killing people."

"We all have to do things we don't like, and killing is one of them."

I walked out of his office, packed my bags, and headed straight to the airport. I came home to West Paterson for the 1972 family Thanksgiving at Aunt Marcella's house.

I know now that the family was suspicious about my visit. Mom asked my brother Tom to have a talk with me. We drove around in his car, and I told him the story, ending with, "A few days ago, I refused to train, and now I am home for Thanksgiving because I am AWOL again." He tried to talk some sense into me, but he was smart enough to know that my mind was made up.

Once again, I was taking a little break to fill my gas tank and make a few navigational corrections to get the raft back into the center of the current for my return. I had no plan other than to return to the fort and face the music. I knew in advance from other privates I'd met who were acting out in their own various ways to get out of the army that AWOL is not the same as Desertion. A soldier needs to be "absent without leave" for thirty days before he is considered a deserter.

I stayed for about ten days before I decided it was time to return. The good news was that, during the holiday, cousin Jimmy had sold me a 1965 Dodge van with a new motor. It was perfect to get me back to the army post seven hundred miles south. I drove through the night and past the front gates of the fort around nine a.m.

Knowing in advance that I was about to enter the as-yet-unknown Return Canyon, I was not looking forward to facing the, "killing is one of the things we all don't like to do" captain. Lucky for me, I had a few Valiums I had taken from my mother's bottle before I left the house and I had popped them about an hour before. Never had I taken these pills, but I did know that my mother liked them because they helped "soothe her nerves." I trusted or hoped they would soothe mine. I parked the van and reported directly to the new captain's office, whereupon his office staff informed me that I was to report back to my old captain.

When I got there, I was as mellow as mellow as can be. I was sitting in the office, waiting, when the office sergeant informed me that there would be no need to report to the captain because they had decided they were letting me out of the army! No one yelled at me, and in a few moments, I was politely told to report back in the morning to receive the paperwork. Wow! Can you imagine the relief?

I had about twenty-four hours to absorb the good news before I actually received the discharge papers. It was after breakfast. I read the words "Undesirable Discharge" with the same reaction I'd had in the beginning, when I had read the word "Infantry." I got upset on the spot, and the extra-calm waters I'd experienced over the previous twenty-four hours vanished.

This was an outcome I had not considered seriously. I had avoided jail, but I had also wanted to avoid an undesirable or dishonorable discharge. Bad school grades were one thing; I had learned early to accept the Ds and Fs, but a bad army discharge was a stigma that lay heavily upon a soldier in the subconscious of the people I'd grown up with. The belief that a bad discharge would follow you the rest of your life had been etched into the stone walls of our culture long before my time.

I read more, after the initial shock, to discover I had the right to challenge my discharge in two ways. In both cases, I had the option to see an army JAG officer (lawyer). Some soldiers receiving this paperwork might not want to leave the service, so they would get a lawyer and hope to win a second chance to stay. My plan was to appeal to the court for a better discharge.

A huge fork in the river was up ahead, and there was plenty of time to move to one side or the other. At least, the pressure was off. I had zero to lose by trying to get a better discharge. In my mind, an "undesirable" discharge held images of bad boys, drug dealers, guys who stole weapons or bullets. I rejected taking these images upon myself. I just wanted out and had been told I had to do something wrong in order to do that, and hell, I was responding to a bet from a major!

I made the appointment for some legal counsel. Like the social worker, this JAG officer also had been drafted and was serving his two years as an officer-lawyer. He wanted to help.

I said, "I want out of the army, but I don't think I deserve an Undesirable Discharge. He was there to help me out, and almost immediately, he spoke of an army regulation that I was unaware of. It stated: "If a soldier is not promoted from private to private first class within the first six months, he is to be considered unfit for military duty and becomes eligible for discharge."

This was our ace in the hole, and it came up almost before the game had started. However, before that card was played, we would have to present our case in front of a board of five officers—three captains and two majors.

I flashed back to basic training graduation day, when one of the company drill sergeants had pulled me off to the side and said he was shocked that the master drill sergeant in charge of my platoon hadn't given me a promotion after I won the PT test. Always, he said, that person gets promoted to first class. Now, it had become a blessing in disguise.

The JAG officer listened to my story from beginning to end and said, "We are going to have to tell them the truth." In other words, we couldn't make shit up. I was not a thief or a drug dealer. Those were the guys who got the undesirable discharges."

On the day of court, the JAG officer and I sat in front of the board. First, my lawyer presented our case. He wove my story into a picture that the board could see and that hopefully would make the case that Private Carroll should be given a general discharge because he was not a thief or a bad guy.

In fact, Private Carroll was a good guy who had entered the army with the attitude of doing his best. He'd proved that when he received the basic training physical fitness award, and yet, that was where the problem had started. The army had made a mistake when they failed to give Private Carroll the one-bar promotion he should have received along with the trophy. The lawyer then spoke of an army regulation which stated that a soldier who has not received a promotion after six months should be discharged because he is not fit for military service, and that this was not necessarily a bad thing. It was, however, a reality that not every male has the capacity to adapt to military life. He spoke of my spiritual/religious feelings and how they related to being unfit for military life, and then he presented the letter from the doctor who'd predicted that if I was not let out of the army, I might act out in multiple ways.

He concluded that at the time of the hearing, Private Carroll had only been in the army for 178 days, whereas the magic number of days a soldier needs is 193 to become eligible for military benefits. (The GI College Bill, for one example). He made the case that all the army had to do was discharge me within the next two weeks, and I would not be eligible for certain government benefits.

Then it was my time to answer questions. This was one of those magical moments when everything becomes so clear that you have no trouble speaking your mind. Previously, I had told the shrink, "It's a feeling or a pressure in my head." On that day, however, I never once struggled for words to answer their questions. The questions I most related to were those about "not wanting to be trained to kill." They came at me from several angles, asking what I might do in certain situations if I, or my family, were under some form of attack. Always, I answered that I would defend the space if it were violated.

It all happened so quickly. When I spoke, it seemed that the clear Voice was uttering the words that came out of my mouth.

The JAG officer and I were told to leave the room while the board deliberated. We waited twenty minutes tops before we were called back to hear the verdict.

"Private Carroll, you are awarded a General Discharge under Honorable Conditions."

The words are hard to find that can describe the feelings that coursed through me, the joy, relief, and pride I felt for getting through this treacherous section of the river while still receiving the general discharge, were blissful. Now, I just had to wait for the formal discharge.

After the trial, the intensity of the normal fort activity started to quiet down. It was getting close to the Christmas holidays, and everyone who had a home to go to left the post. Those few privates who remained were asked to consolidate into a few rooms in one barrack instead of remaining scattered throughout several buildings.

So, who do you think ended up in the bunk next to me? The guy who had punched me in the mouth! It was a little weird, and certainly I would not have picked the bunk next to his if I'd had a choice, but for some reason I didn't move to another bunk. Sometime later, we were in the bathroom together. These are big bathrooms with lots of sinks and toilets and plenty of room to move around and talk. It was there that the guy pulled out a good-size switchblade from his pocket and started cleaning his nails. We were making some small talk. He wondered what my family house looked like when I was growing up and how many bedrooms and bathrooms there were. When I described my house on Fritz Lane, he was taken aback and admitted that he'd assumed I had a much bigger and nicer house.

He was a ghetto boy who had never left until he went into the army. Growing up where we white boys were told never to go, he surely hadn't ever visited a place like West Paterson or attended a school like PV.

It was our fate to meet again in calmer waters where there was room and time to communicate. He said that he had joined the army to get out of the city. He showed me the wound in his leg where a bullet had passed through when he was shot in the "hood." After he told me that, I said, "That three-on-one fight wasn't fair!" He laughed and told me that, where he came from, all that mattered was, "We beat the whitey."

I had grown up playing by a beautiful brook and I'd had the chance to play every sport I wanted to. He had grown up in the hard and ugly ghetto, where, he said, "For fun as eight-year-olds, we would cut school and get drunk in the alleys."

We became friends. Maybe I was the first white person he'd met who didn't feel negative towards him, or maybe we had gotten through the "black-and-white" issue and seen each other with respect after the fight. Or could it be because it was our first Christmas away from home? I don't know.

Late during our Christmas holiday, he was getting something out of his locker before he headed to the shower when he looked over at me and said, "I don't have to worry about my locker being open, I trust you." Can you imagine? This guy had told me in the past that he didn't trust anyone when it came to his money and material possessions, and I had assured him that he was correct to think that way. Yet, now he trusted me! It was a beautiful thing. I was at peace; the river was widening and straightening to the point that I could see my way home.

I had my van and was free leave Fort Jackson to visit the town. Often, I visited the University of South Carolina campus and hung out in the coffee shop or took drives in the country. It was a mellow period. I simply waited for my discharge.

Once, on the way to Myrtle Beach for the weekend with a friend, I was pulled over by the State Police. The cop was nice and simply reminded me that I was driving too long in the left lane. He set me free without a ticket. When I returned to the van, I told my friend that everything was okay. He smiled, and I saw nothing but black teeth. In his fear of getting busted by the cops, he had eaten the hunk of hash we had planned to smoke at the beach. We laughed hard while he got very stoned.

It was not until the morning of January 12th, 204 days after being drafted, I received my court verdict: "General Discharge under Honorable Conditions."

I walked out of the captain's office, tossed my duffel bag in the van, fired up the motor, and started driving towards the exit. Just as the van was nearing the big gate with its armed guards, I pushed the cassette tape into the player deck and heard Jim Morrison of The Doors, singing, "I've been down so Goddamn long that it looks like up to me," and drove through Fort Jackson's gates a free man!

Chapter 5:
EVERYTHING IS WITHIN

I was on a pure adrenalin buzz as I turned the van north and drove seven hundred miles straight back to West Paterson.

Friends were happy to see me back, but there would be no party to celebrate my return. In fact, it soon became clear that nothing much had changed in my home or within my circle of friends. There I was, back down in the basement, listening to my stereo as if nothing had changed during the past six months.

But, of course, things had changed. For example, the dividing bridge was long gone. Physically, I was back in my hometown, but mentally, I was somewhere else. The Military River Canyon experience had altered the energetics of my life in several ways. It had taken me way out into my mind; I was like a kite on a string, riding high in the sky. Now, I had to figure out how to get the kite back without crashing it into a tree or snapping the string?

Back in the 1960s, when we kids were lucky enough to get the perfect wind, our kite would fly many hundreds of feet into the sky. However, because our hillside neighborhood consisted of jutting houses and congested trees, we could never hope to reel it back in once we got it up that high. On those special days, the paper kite with its home-made cloth tail might fly for hours on a steady breeze. When the breeze increased enough to snap the string or faded enough for the kite to crash, it was time for the owner to roam the area on a kite search. Like that, I was way out there, flying high in the winds over South Carolina as the buzz wore off and I started my descent (although I didn't know it at the time), while my feet were on the ground back in West Paterson.

Several weeks after my return, Steve and I decided to go skiing in northern Vermont.

As on our Florida trip, hotels were not in our budget. The plan was to sleep in Steve's 1964 Ford Econoline van. We knew that it would be cold but had never considered just how cold eighteen degrees below zero would be at five a.m. when the motor wouldn't start. We managed not to freeze to death, and by mid-morning, someone gave us a jumpstart in time for us to get to the slopes. By afternoon we were exhausted and in need of a shower. It was our luck to discover a local hotel with an attached spa that was open to the general public for a reasonable price. For several hours, we padded back and forth between the sauna and the hot tub. Refreshed, we ate dinner and headed for the nearest nightclub.

• • •

I'll admit that finding a girl who wanted to have sex was certainly on my mind. Well, it was my lucky night; I found a girl willing to go out into the van on that cold night and play around. So, I had this nice lady in the van under the covers with no clothes on, and I suddenly became aware that I was not and had not been feeling any sexual energy. It just wasn't there in the form of physical arousal. The desire had been all in my mind and had not transferred to my body. Realizing this was a shock to my system, as if I had been tossed into icy-cold water. In fact, I was in the water and holding on to the side ropes of the raft when I had a limp ejaculation release that was a total shock and insult to my ego.

I apologized and was grateful that not another word was spoken, because I was freaking out. If I had thought before that life was moving fast, this incident felt like getting swept into the mighty Passaic River on the 55-gallon-drum raft. And worse, it happened again the next night! This time, by the grace of the gods, it happened without the girl's knowledge, and I simply acted as if I were completely exhausted and needed to sleep.

By morning, we'd had enough of Vermont's cold. As we drove back to Jersey, I didn't speak a word to Steve about my little mishap. Internally, however, I was ramped up. I could not hear the clear, calm, and reassuring Voice, and I could no longer maintain my grip on the side rope of my raft. I was shivering with cold and tumbling through the rapids, seeing no possible way to reach my raft or the shore anytime soon.

Back home at some point, I visited my doctor, the same doctor who had taken care of me throughout high school. I told him the problem. He asked what was happening in my life. He took my blood pressure. Without telling me what it was, he exclaimed, "You are high strung! There is too much going on inside your head." He asked what kinds of drugs I was using. I told him the short version of my tale, and he said, "Weed is okay, but stay away from the mind-altering drugs." Then he gave me a prescription for some pills to fix my problem.

The sun was shining when I walked out of the office. I was filled with hope. However, these were not the magic erectile pills we see advertised in our present day. These old pills did not produce the desired results. The doctor had been right. My overly active mind had grabbed 100 percent of my attention, and I had not had time or space to let anyone into my life. How can anyone have a relationship when they are trying to keep themselves from drowning or are, like I was, on an expedition to find their lost kite? My mind was in serious trouble as I realized I had lost contact with the Voice.

Thinking about it now, I see that, upon my discharge, I lost my intense mental focus on getting out of the army, and it created a huge, internal void. Everything that had captured my attention for the last seven months suddenly disappeared, just as the kite did when the string snapped. Like a boy searching for his lost kite, I was searching for the internal voice above all else.

It makes sense; but back then, I had no clue as to why my body didn't respond properly, and I was definitely not interested in sharing ideas or asking for advice.

After many weeks of struggle and wandering around, I finally saw a piece of my kite string—no kite, just string—but a welcome sign, a note of sorts from the Voice. And so, I slowly started to come back into my body. I could hear the Voice in the distance, and at the same time feel my feet touch the ground. I continued my search with a renewed energy, reassured that I was on a track that was leading me to myself. The tension and stress eased just a bit.

It was a rough winter. Only by the grace of unemployment benefits was I able to live comfortably in my parents' basement, where I began to get hold of myself.

In late March, Steve and I decided to drive south and soak up some of the warm Florida sun. Images of my Spring Break experience from the year before filled my head. A ray of sunlight broke through the sky as we drove south in a Ford van.

The crowds of Spring Break had not yet arrived, but there were people on the beach, and I was on a mission to find a happy face. I had no interest in having a sexual encounter.

It didn't take long before I bumped into a girl from New York, who was reading a book, The Teachings of Don Juan, by Carlos Castaneda. After a little introduction, she started telling me about it and continued to hold my attention until she lent me the book for the afternoon. It was the first time in my life I didn't want to put a book down. As the Moody Blues did, this book spoke to my inner awareness.

This was the kind of information I had been craving, but without knowing it. The story and teachings helped me make sense of what I was experiencing. It was an introduction to the world of Shamanism that introduced the tonal and nagual parts of ourselves, as well as the four natural enemies of man. These terms denote the two "parallel" worlds that comprise the universe: the material world of objects, which includes our bodies (tonal) and the non-material world (nagual).

We have the tonal (the entire physical world, which includes our body), and we also have the nagual (our consciousness of everything, which could also be called spirit, thoughts, emotions, feelings, urges, visions, beliefs, etc.). The point is that we are equally responsible for our actions in the physical world (the tonal) and in the world of consciousness (the nagual).

Don Juan's four natural enemies of man are fear, clarity, power, and old age.

For the first time in my life, I felt inspired to purchase a book. The impact of The Teachings of Don Juan astounded me. Never before had a book spoken to me so clearly. The words spoke directly to my struggling mind and made perfect sense. I had been like someone forcing my way through a dense jungle, and now a pathway had appeared, leading to teachings relevant to dealing with, and moving around, in the non-physical world without losing your kite or getting flipped out of your raft.

• • •

Soon after returning from Florida, I got a job as a laborer/carpenter in the ever-expanding New Jersey suburbs. We could frame a house in less than three days. We always kept busy. There was never time for talking. If anyone talked too much, the boss would say, "Back to work. Got to make coffee money!" It was the perfect job for me at that time. I learned quickly, and the hard physical work gave my mind a natural rest that allowed my mind to begin reconnecting with my body.

I worked forty hours a week for the next three months, and during that time, I more or less got my shit together again. I got hold of my raft and managed to climb back in just before entering the next canyon.

The Voice said: "It's time to move out of New Jersey."

I had a van with a wood platform bed, a Coleman cook stove, and a few hundred bucks. Myrtle Beach was on my mind. The day I left home, I kissed my mother goodbye. She had tears in her eyes. I didn't know what was in front of me, but I knew I needed to go.

It was a straight drive to the hotel where Cousin Jimmy worked along the Myrtle Beach strip. I knew that the owner of the hotel parking lot would be cool about letting me spend a few nights parked there before he decided I was a free loader, and this allowed for a soft landing. A few days later, however, I felt pressured to find somewhere to stay. My first choice was to visit the place where Steve and I had stayed two years earlier.

The landlady remembered me. All the rooms were booked for the next month, but let me park up against a sand dune, where the van's double doors opened up to the beach.

I was allowed to use the bunkhouse toilet and the outdoor shower. The photo shows the exact spot where I parked the van. It was the corner spot closest to the state park and beach. The bunkhouses are now gone.

It was a dream come true. Everything was perfect: the weather, the people who visited, and me getting hired to cut the grass and do odds and ends in exchange for rent.

My location allowed me to see just about everyone who visited the bunkhouses, and within days, I adapted to my new life as if it would never end. I felt "high on the world." In Shamanic terms, my tonal life was completely content living in a van on the beach. For the first time, I had no set plan for my future: no school, no army, and no job.

Often soldiers on leave from Fort Bragg, North Carolina, found their way to the bunkhouse for R and R. Of these, a few returned often enough during that summer that we became friends.

The most memorable soldier to visit the bunkhouse was a guy named Ray. The first time we met, he was on sick leave due to a gun blast near his eardrum. With him, I tripped on acid and saw my first tracer: we were playing with a football on the beach. After it was kicked, the football tumbled through the air, and a clear replica of the football followed it. No big deal, but it was exciting to finally see a tracer after reading and hearing stories about them. By then, I had tripped about twenty times on what people called acid, orange sunshine, windowpane, Mr. Natural, and the like. Until seeing the tracer, I had never witnessed anything out of the ordinary visually, although tripping in Mother Nature was always the most pleasurable and beautiful.

Ray always had something good to take or smoke. After the football-tracer trip, we had something I remember as Cannabinol in pill form. It was natural and gave a calm, peaceful high. During this trip, Ray looked me in the eye and said, "You're still searching, aren't you? You really don't know, do you?"

It was the first time someone had seen me as I was on the inside. He was right; I didn't know. I asked a lot of questions that some people didn't like, but I was most surely searching for more relevant information relating to this "life thing" that was going on inside and out.

On Ray's next visit, he had what he called LSD 25. I had no idea what that meant. I had tripped before but had never heard of LSD 25. This time, instead of putting the little tab in our mouths, we decided to boil it in Kool-Aid first, and then drink it. Moments after we swallowed the last drop of the Kool-Aid, another friend who had just taken LSD assured us that boiling the Kool-Aid made all the acid go up in the steam—and he did not want to trip alone—so we took another hit.

It was halfway between sunset and darkness when I first realized I was getting off. There was a buzz in my ear, and the normal darkness that usually engulfs the planet at sunset wasn't happening, yet the sand was glowing with its own light.

The high was coming on fast as I walked through the sand dune to the beach and saw the ocean. The waves were gone! Instead, where the normal white foam at the edge of the waves moves in and out, a light appeared, but it was not going in and out, it was going up and down! It looked something like an irritating static sound wave on a television monitor. I got nervous when I noticed that the static light waves and the sound were related to what I was feeling. As I became more nervous, the waves and the sound seemed to get louder, bigger, faster, and more chaotic!

I turned and looked for Ray, who was laughing and joking around with some others.

As if I were launching into one of those forked canyons, without hesitation I walked straight up to Ray and said, "What the fuck is happening?"

He laughed. "Oh, you never tripped like this before? Ha!" We walked away from the gathering together, heading south into the deserted state park.

Ray began to explain, as he lit a cigarette and spun the glow of its red tip around in circles so we could see the completed circle of light.

No big deal; every child learns that trick when they spin a flashlight or sparkler in the dark. But then, we looked up at the stars on this moonless night and noticed that the light of each star appeared to be spinning in tiny circles. It reminded me of looking at the night sky with a pair of binoculars; the stars spin until your hands become steady or you place the viewing piece on a tripod for stability.

Then, Ray increased the range of motion of his arm, thereby increasing the size diameter of the spinning circle of light circle from the cigarette, and then flung his hand up towards the sky. The once-spinning circle stretched into a light beam that shot into the heavens and connected to the spinning light of the brightest star in the sky. I kid you not. In his hand, he still held a visible beam of light that now extended from his cigarette to the star!

I was transfixed by what I was seeing. I didn't know what to make of it when he turned and handed me the cigarette. Immediately, I reached out my hand and, like a firm handshake, I felt the power from the light beam enter my hand to the point that it required physical strength to hold on, similar to holding a powerful fire hose. My eyes followed the light to the star.

Speechless and mesmerized, I couldn't respond to the question Ray kept repeating: "Where does this come from?"

I finally said, "I have no idea!"

"It is all within you," he replied.

Then, we turned our attention to the waves. The chaotic up-and-down motion of light waves and sound had mellowed. Now, the waves moved in and out with the slow rhythmic motion and sound one might find on a moonless, windless night at low tide.

I was so blown way away that I ask Ray straight out, "Are you from outer space?" I was totally serious.

He laughed and said, "You judged me by the length of my hair!"

We started walking south, the moving light beam of waves beneath our feet.

With just the snap of a finger, Ray picked up one of the light waves. He held it in his hand and wiggled it. Imagine holding on to the nozzle of a watering hose with an endless stream of water. Now, imagine moving the nozzle with your hand and notice how this alters the stream's pattern. This is what he was doing with the light as he made it dance out in front of us.

Once again, my attention was riveted on the light. This time, he didn't hand me the beam as he had done with the cigarette. Instead, he instructed me on how to grab it.

"See the beam while at the same time feeling the beam in your hand. Feel it in your fingertips as they extend from your hand and arm toward the light. It's as if you waded into a river and stood in water just deep enough to let your fingers touch it, but instead of water, there was light down by your feet. If you open your hand and consciously expand it with your muscles, you will notice it gets bigger until you relax, and then it goes back to its normal size. That's kind of what I was doing when I first made the connection. Even though my fingers were neither hot nor cold, they started tingling. The light wave was responding to the motion of my hands. Then I could see it rising up, and the next moment, it was in my grasp!"

So there we stood, both holding and moving our individual light beams around as if they were magic light ropes that stretched out as far as the eyes could see. Any motion of the hand would send the light rippling out.

It is hard to say how long we walked and danced with the light in our hands before we stopped to talk. Ray told me that the body and mind are one, and that it is here in the oneness that the masters of martial arts, such as Bruce Lee, get their powers.

I could see that my hands looked and felt as if they were filled with steel ball bearings, yet at the same time, they moved with lightning swiftness. This is how the masters use their hands to break through a seemingly impossible thickness of wood or pile of bricks. For a while, I marveled at the speed and power I was experiencing in my body.

As we sat down and looked out over the ocean, once again I could understand how the power worked at its most basic level. What I had felt was reflected in the sound and motion of the light waves. The oneness that I had only sensed previously was now confirmed for me as literal reality.

Everything was calm and peaceful until I started to remember the Michael with a van and a room in the bunkhouse, who earlier that year had been released from the army. Thinking these thoughts and feeling the small wave of fear that accompanied them caused the gently moving light waves to increase in both speed and noise.

Imagine peacefully sitting at the edge of a perfectly still mountain lake and looking out across the water. There, a mountain valley shows the movement and sound of wind on the trees, working its way down toward the lake. Imagine that you begin to see ripples coming towards you from across the water. Soon, your body feels the wind and perceives that the intensity of the wind and sound are directly related to the ripples on the once-flat surface of the lake.

Imagine, now, that when you consciously think disturbing, fear-filled thoughts, you are simultaneously creating internal winds. These winds ripple or wave out into the world and are directly related to the quality of the thoughts you hold. Perhaps you have heard the saying, "No negative waves!" People say that because negative waves can directly influence both your own experience and the experience of others.

It is an unavoidable reality of being human. Nothing is hidden from those who can see and hear. Our human eyes and ears are extremely limited when it comes to the visible light and sound spectrum.

It must have been two a.m., and I had been "tripping my ass off," as we used to say, in this world of light for hours when I had my first conscious recognition that I was very high. That realization was accompanied by the winds of past memories. The light waves began to speed up slowly, like an old-fashioned steam engine picking up speed as it leaves the station.

Ray laughed in his in gentle way and commented that we were beginning to come down. His only instructions were, "Try to remember everything you can, because the next part is going to be like hell."

He suggested we have a few tokes to ease our way down. The toke on the weed worked wonders to calm my waves of fear. Soon, we got up and started walking toward the light waves again.

On the Google map, we can see that the distance between the dunes and the water is perhaps a hundred feet, just a thirty-second walk to the water's edge. We walked toward the light waves for what could have been ten minutes or half an hour—in other words, it took a while before we realized that, after a certain point, we never got any closer to the light waves. We had been walking as if we were on a treadmill. This seemed to surprise even Ray. We laughed for a moment, and he said, "This is a preview of what the point is, which is to get here naturally; drugs are not the answer."

On the way back to the bunkhouse, we noticed that our arms were turning a silver-gray. "We are coming down and burning like space capsules reentering the Earth's atmosphere," he said.

Everything was still glowing in its astral light when we returned to the bunkhouse. When I touched the metal lock to open the door, it vibrated in my hand like a gentle electric current. By then, I was no longer excited. Everything felt meaningless. My body felt heavy, as if something were weighing me down. I managed to get to my bed before I collapsed. This had nothing to do with a need to fall asleep. I was wide-awake and feeling the most severe and pressing loneliness that I had ever felt. Looking at Ray, who was leaning up against the wall, I asked, "Are you the devil?" Like the alien question, I was serious. He just laughed in a mild manner. He knew where my head was and understood that nothing anyone could say at this time would make it better.

My bedside window looked out upon the wilds of the state park's grassy sand dunes. Now, however the reeds and tall grasses were all aglow and bubbling like those old-fashioned liquid Christmas tree bubble lights we had when I was a kid. A thought grabbed my attention. I remembered that Carlos Castaneda had talked about an experience similar to mine in his book. Finally, I had come down enough to have a memory. A foot had finally touched down and come in contact with the bottom of the river after a rough go, which helped bring back the light of hope from deep within. Slowly, the weight I was feeling started to lift, and I was able to get up off the bed.

When I left the room, Ray appeared to be sleeping. I walked downstairs and went outside.

Looking up at the sky, and from a very deep place, I spoke out loud, "God help me!"

Instantly, a wave of comfort came upon my being. I could no longer see the light wave, but the feeling was as present as it had been in the middle of the night. By the time I walked from the bunkhouse to the dunes, my dog Surf appeared beside me. We walked to the water's edge. I sat down, looked out at the thin line where the ocean meets the sky, and at exactly that moment, the sun began to rise.

Another day had begun.

• • •

I know now that our thoughts, be they hidden in silence or spoken aloud, actually affect our environment. In our normal world, we often refer to this as a person's vibe. Even if we can't see it, we can feel it.

I also know that sometimes a person can master the art of the vibe, like a good actor playing his role, and use it to fool others. In other words, it is power that can be used for selfish reasons.

Ray had been speaking about the power of positive thinking and how important it is to be positive, because the power behind positive thoughts can hold back or defuse the crazy, static-fear waves. We will receive whatever our highly focused thoughts reflect, for better or worse. Both the devil and the saint draw their power from the same well. The outcome is determined by how that power is directed and used.

The warning that Ray had given me on my way down—that I was about to enter hell—didn't help to ward off the experience or make it any easier. He was simply expressing the fact that there would be a price to pay for such a trip. On the way down, I was stripped of all the power I had felt and held in my hands and mind at the peak of the trip. It felt like death to my ego. For a time while I had lain on the bed, I had felt no spirit. I had felt only empty and hopelessly adrift in eternity.

Remembering the story from Don Juan and the bubble lights had been the first threads to reconnecting my personality back into my body. When I reached out and said, "God help me!" my spirit came back.

The floodgates and filters in my mind had been blown open. For the next few days, I found it hard to sleep. There was so much to remember. I wrote in my notebook and spoke to anyone who would listen. I had experienced another world and come back to tell all who would listen!

Michael Carroll

Chapter 6:
AFTER THE LIGHT - HEADING SOUTH

It would be an understatement to say that I had become a motor-mouth after the Kool-Aid trip. I was so full of desire to share it with everyone that it was almost impossible to keep my mouth shut.

Some people thought I was crazy and some felt I was pushy; others listened. This compulsion continued for the next few weeks, peaking out on Labor Day weekend with the last full house of the summer season. Come Tuesday morning, I was the only one living in the bunkhouse. I accepted the landlady's offer to rent the small, one-room apartment on the first floor that had a bath and a very small kitchen for the same price I had been paying. The weekends still attracted vacationers, but it was so boring that after a week I was willing to accept a fulltime job as a laborer with a company that was building the local outdoor wastewater treatment plant. The job consisted mostly of placing plastic pipes in the pit that would soon be filled with human wastewater.

Sometime around mid-September, and just a few days after I had started working, my friend Jeffery stopped by to visit on his drive back to Gainesville, where he was to be entering his senior year at the University of Florida. He was a fellow pole vaulter, cross-country runner, and card-playing gambler from high school. Jeff had time to hang with me for some days before he continued south, and by the time he was ready to leave, I had quit my job and was ready to follow him south in my van.

Over the summer, Jeffery had decided to return to Gainesville but not to attend school. The city welcomed fifty thousand students every year and was considered such a cool place to live that many stayed there after dropping out or graduating.

Jeff had a room on the second floor of a big old house that was within walking distance of the university. He let me sleep on the floor, and we were allowing things to unfold from there. The number-one priority in my mind, once my sleeping mat and bag were on floor, was to find some LSD and trip with Jeffery so I could show him what I had learned. Jeff was no rookie went it came to tripping. In fact, we had tripped on windowpane up near Hunter Mountain in New York state sometime in June before I left for Myrtle Beach. We had spent the day there playing in a mountain stream. The water level was the perfect height to expose smooth, river-rock surfaces that Mother Nature had placed perfectly so that we could literally step, run, or skip from one stone to another up and down the mountain canyon. There had been five-, ten-, and fifteen-foot waterfalls with deep pools below, which we could jump or dive into. Yes, tripping during the day in Mother Nature was always nice.

In a few days, we located two hits of windowpane. This time, there would be no LSD 25 in the Kool-Aid; we placed the tabs on our tongues.

When it started getting dark, we left the house and walked over to the small city park. By the time we reached the park, the green-grass light was just coming on. This time, there were no obvious white-foam waves of light. Instead, there were energy tubes of green light that I could see rising up out of the now-glowing green grass. The wavy tubes extended out across the lawn in a similar way that the waves had extended along the shoreline.

It was time. In my power-of-positive-thinking mode, I started to focus on the light beams while working my hands in the same way that I had when I pulled up the wave on the beach. It didn't take long to stir up the energy. However, unlike the ocean waves, which stayed constant in one direction up and down along the coast, the green-grass energy was all around me, as if I were standing in the center of a large pond of moving energy.

The energy had a snakelike quality as it moved through the grass; it had no head or tail, and it didn't feel like a snake in my hands; the energy was simply there to be seen and felt as it started to vibrate in a way similar to that of the static light waves at the beginning of my Kool-Aid trip.

Now, think of the data that travels through the airwaves and into our wireless cell phones and computers. It is invisible. Somehow, words, photos, and videos magically pass through the walls of our house and into our computers without being seen. Things are just not as solid as they appear to the naked eye. The human eye sees at best only 3 percent of the known light spectrum (also referred to as the electromagnetic spectrum), and that is just the "known spectrum." (An example of other known spectrums that are present but not visible to the naked eye are cosmic rays, gamma rays, x-rays, radio and microwaves, infrared, and ultraviolet.)

Jeff looked at me. He could see what I was doing and said, "You're like Don Juan." Right away, I knew I wasn't like Don Juan and that I didn't know anything about what I was grabbing onto, other than the fact that it was there.

This was one of those sections of rapids where you know you are in way over your head. You know that you've been here before, that you have capsized and come close to drowning. Now, you get to deal with a similar situation and find out if you can get through it, this time without getting flipped.

A wave of fear shifted my intensity and focus away from my original plan. This wasn't fun. I recognized right away that I was in a serious situation. I was almost out of the boat and in the water with no one there to save me but myself. I walked away from Jeff.

As I continued walking, I considered how I was going to show him anything when I was beginning to freak out. I was doing my best to hold down the rising light energy by taking my finger and pointing it down at the energy field at my feet, at the same time saying in a loud, firm voice, "Get down! Get down!" the way a person yells a command to an aggressive dog. It was a technique I had learned from Ray for holding the energy at bay when it was getting out of control. Surely, someone who could not see what I was seeing would think I was crazy.

Alone, I walked the quiet, neighborhood streets in the light of night until I noticed from a distance a guy and a girl walking together. Without question or hesitation, I walked straight up to them and said, "I am having a hard time on acid and could use a little help." They were not surprised and seemed to take it in stride.

They said, "Oh, we've been there before," and invited me to walk with them to a nearby park. We sat on the grass at the edge of a pond while they told stories about the lives of holy men and I listened.

After what seemed to be a few hours, the guy said, "You think you're okay, now?"

"Yes," I said. I was in calmer water and grateful for the wisdom these two souls had used to soothe my fears. We parted with a bow and went our ways.

I was still in the light, but all the energy swirls had receded back into the grass, or perhaps I just stopped focusing on them. Either way, I was not in the dark. The street signs were pillars aglow with their own light, as was everything else. There were no shadows.

By dawn, I had fully come down from my high.

Back to regular living, it took me only a few weeks to realize that living in an old college housing district with six or eight others was not for me.

• • •

By another stroke of luck, Jeff and I met Jill, who wanted to sell a trailer sitting on five acres in the country about ten miles west of Gainesville for eight hundred dollars. It was in a one-gas-station, convenience-store town known as Jonesville, Florida

It was a funky trailer on its last legs. It had cold water, a toilet, a cold shower, and a refrigerator, sink, and stove. The rent for the land was twenty-nine dollars a month. Divided by two of us, that was fourteen-fifty each, plus five dollars or so for half the electric. It meant I could live on a hundred bucks a month, including food.

I had met a guy named Clay Jones at the college house. He was older, and by that, I mean he was thirty to my twenty-one. He invited me to walk over to the health food store with him. Like an older brother, Clay shared his knowledge of nutrition, and I first became aware of a vegetarian diet.

His rap was so convincing that by the time we got to the store, I had converted. That day, I took the first steps toward understanding what my new diet would be. I absorbed many lessons about eating in a healthy way and about a new idea called fasting.

October was harvest season for a small farm near our trailer, so on the way home one day, I stopped by to pick up some fresh veggies. On that day, I purchased red beets. I tried to eat one raw, like a carrot. It was not the greatest, as I remember, but it was the first of many experiments.

The next morning, we headed out to a place known as "the sinkhole," a circle of big trees, in the middle of which was a hole in the ground a beautiful, small pond perhaps thirty feet down. Local legend says that it is the entrance to underwater caves that just meander on and on and eventually connect to other underground waterways. I went down the pathway to the pond. After a while, I had to take a piss. Standing on a big rock, I turned away from the water and let it go. There was blood in my piss! A stream of red piss arched its way out and down to the ground. Freaked out, I went right away to the free health clinic at the university. They couldn't find anything wrong and sent me on my way. I am not sure how many more years it took before I connected the dots between the raw beets and red piss!

Another time, after fasting on fruit for three days, I broke the fast by eating a can of salted cashews. The resulting stomach and intestinal pains were bad enough, but the experience was made even worse because I happened to be camping in Cousin Jimmy's van while parked at Hunter Mountain Ski Resort in New York on a frigid winter night.

Number-one rule: It doesn't make sense to go on a three-day fruit fast before a winter camping expedition; and second, when breaking a fast, always eat something soft and easy to digest.

Clay was a guitar player and a friend of the owner of the New Harvest Health Food Restaurant. It was there, among those two friends, that the idea was born to turn the restaurant into a music venue on Friday and Saturday nights for the fall season of 1973. Clay booked the acts and coordinated the show. I collected money at the door for ten bucks a night and a free meal. Like cutting the grass once a week for free rent on the beach, this was a good deal considering I could live thinly on twenty bucks a week.

Many great musicians played there during the next few months, but one show stood out above all the rest. On this particular Friday night, I was sick as a dog, but I still went to work. Playing that night was a band from Taos, New Mexico, called The Heart Glow Trio. They sang beautiful songs about love and light as the spiritual reality. In between the songs, they spoke of their teacher/guru Herman Rednick. By evening's end, I was 100 percent healed, feeling great, and convinced that it had to do with the powerful healing energy of the band.

In fact, Robert, a friend who was visiting from Jersey, was so taken by the music that within the next few weeks, he packed his bag and moved to Taos to meet the guru.

. . .

The fall weather in northern Florida that year was so absolutely perfect that it seemed that summer vacation never ended. I worked two evenings, and the rest of the week was open and free of commitments.

Country living was similar to living on the beach. It satisfied the tonal, or physical, part of my life, and yet it left lots of room for the nagual, the unseen, to make itself known. At the beach, a few people were around during most of the day, and there was always the pleasure of walking south through the state park and north up to the pavilion, where people gathered later in the evening. Country living, by contrast, takes "facing our solitude" to a whole new level.

I was deep into my own thoughts and trying to do my best to enjoy my ride, and yet, I was keenly aware of the rapids I was riding, which took me to places high and low. I would enter places of bliss when I was high on the waves for days, and then somehow the waves would flip me out of the raft and into a hole, where I was forced to struggle and seek help to understand what was going on."

During those months, I got hooked on reading certain kinds of books. Be Here Now, by Ram Dass, was a mainstay, especially the brown pages in the middle of the book. I began to understand that others had passed this way before me. And the bottom of page 39 spoke directly to the ups and downs of the rapids:

> You've been really working on yourself and
>
> you're very pure and something very high
>
> happens to you and you feel liberated and
>
> then…your ego walks around and pats you
>
> on the shoulder saying, "Pretty good! Look
>
> how Holy you're becoming," and then you
>
> fall….again.

I did not consider myself "very pure," but I did have the sense that I was on to something, and the analogy fit perfectly into my circumstances.

Now that the floodgates of my thinking mind were wide open, they were causing a lot of discomfort. That was when I first learned about meditation as a method to calm the mind down. I wondered why no one had spoken a word to me about meditation until then.

During my early exploration of meditation, I was also introduced to the astral plane and other levels of existence/consciousness that are present but generally not visible to the physical eye. I was exposed to the consciousness-expanding concepts of reincarnation and karma. These became clear while I was reading a book called The Ultimate Frontier, by Eklal Kueshana.

Within days of moving into the trailer, I began forcing myself to meditate. That is, I disciplined my body to sit and repeat the mantra

"Om," over and over in my head. It was like tossing an empty plastic water bottle into a flooding arroyo. I would sit and say, "Om-Om-Om-Om-Om," a few times, and then I would be off thinking about something else. The instructions were to do this every day.

After a few weeks of daily meditation, I felt a noticeable difference. My days and nights went more smoothly. If I missed a day of practice, and especially if I missed two days, I could feel my inner river speeding up and a rising fear of being capsized.

Most nights were lonely out in the country with absolutely nothing to do, and they became even lonelier as the days shortened and the nights lengthened. My inner river was often relentless in its speed and noise. Out of sheer desperation, I often walked to the convenience store and purchased a half-gallon of ice cream. It was not unusual for me to eat the whole half-gallon in one or two evenings as a distraction from my overly loud and fast mental activity. If there was no ice cream, lots of pieces of toast with butter and jelly did the trick. Yes, some of it I am sure had to do with my experiment with vegetarianism and a failure to eat regular meals.

Nonetheless, the Kool-Aid had opened the floodgates in my head and overloaded me with energy, realizations, and thoughts. In essence, the LSD-induced experience had opened the naturally-closed, protective filter humans have, our chakras, that normally keep our two worlds separate. My chakras no longer kept 100 percent of the light out.

Of course, we have all heard those stories from the 1960s and 70s about people flipping out on acid. This is how I understand it: These people blew a hole in one or more of the naturally protected energy centers in their physical bodies. By this, I mean that the center remained open after the trip was over. It would be like opening the door of a spaceship to go for a spacewalk and not being able to close it again to keep the oxygen in.

It wasn't that bad for me. I got the door closed, although it was no longer perfectly light-proof. That is, with a little focus, I could still see traces of the light energy coming through the cracks.

Spiritual seekers who had gone "under the bridge," so to speak, and into the unknown converged on Gainesville in great numbers. It seemed that every spiritual consciousness-raising group in the country had a storefront there and were in the market for devotees willing to pay cash for training in how to find enlightenment.

One of the more powerful groups in 1973, The Divine Light Mission, had a young boy as their guru/leader. This group's hook was their self-professed ability to "impart knowledge." The boy guru was rumored to be a reincarnation of Jesus, Buddha, or some other holy man of the past. There was to be a special, three-day event at the Houston Astrodome, where we could hear the guru speak. The gathering was to mark the beginning of one thousand years of peace on Earth.

Jeff and I bought into the hype and made plans to go. When the time arrived, we drove his little car directly to the event in time for the first day of a three-day gathering. The astrodome was built to hold seventy-five thousand people, and this gathering attracted perhaps three or four thousand. Once inside the dome, we had to look across the far end of the artificial grass playing field to see the main stage.

We listened to the speakers for maybe an hour before we caught on to what was happening. The event was more like a political pep rally for the little guru and his mission. There were endless speeches. They went on and on for many hours before the main event of listening to Guru Maharaji.

Soon, we were bored and left the dome; and as it turned out, we were not the only ones. In fact, there were probably more people outside the dome that day than inside, all discussing their diverse life paths. The Jesus freaks were passionate and had come to fulfill a mission, which was to warn about the evil ways of the guru. Hare Krishna devotees were dressed in their gowns as they preached, danced, and sang their songs. Hippie guitar players were playing and singing, while many of those who gathered around to listen talked about their esoteric spiritual beliefs.

There were conversations about reincarnation and what it takes to become "free from birth," and how that relates to karma and consciousness. We didn't know shit; it reminded me of pulling up the light energy tubes in the green grass; we were all just scratching the surface for information.

Several guys arguing about the how, when, and where enlightenment takes place. Finally, a guy who was older, maybe thirty, had had enough. Cutting through the bullshit, he spoke out in a clear tone: "Enlightenment can happen at any time and in any place; in fact, you can reach enlightenment while sitting on a toilet!"

• • •

For Christmas of 1973, I managed to car pool a ride up to Jersey with my dog. If my family thought I was weird after the army, imagine what they would think now, after my LSD experiences.

I had a plan in mind to spread the word: I would tell everyone about my discovery of the light and the oneness of the world. "It's all right here!" I'd say. I would tell everyone about the wonders of not eating meat and of meditation—and more.

In my zealousness to enlighten my family and friends, I encountered a few obstacles. For two weeks, I had an uncontrollable, rambling, motor mouth. I was on a mission to enlighten that backfired.

After New Year's Eve, on the first day of 1974, I crashed from sheer mental exhaustion. The bottom fell out of my boat, and I was swimming in cold, turbulent waters without a life jacket. Why was no one interested? At my bottom, surrounded by tall waves, I opened Be Here Now to the brown page 97 where there is a picture of a guy walking down the center aisle of a church, preaching in all his excitement to everyone, but nobody understood. At the bottom of the page, it says, "Don't be psychotic: Watch it. Watch it." Again, I got the message.

This was a big tumble; and yes, I was repeatedly learning that there was wisdom in keeping my mouth shut. The pain comes from saying something you wish you hadn't said, and then chasing after it even though you know you can never take it back. I wondered how many times it would take to learn this lesson.

Thank the gods, I had books and music to fall back on for inner guidance. Who in New Jersey could have related to me at the time? Scott Spencer was the only guy I could think of, but then again, he was way into The Teachings of Don Juan and all the Castaneda books that followed.

Into the Unknown

• • •

After the holidays, my dad paid for my train ticket south and dropped my dog Surf and me at the train station. I had built a crate big enough for Surf to lie down and sleep on the trip. As a young lab mix with a huge passion to fetch sticks, he had a lot of energy. He couldn't get enough and got his name after I tossed a stick in the ocean and he dove right into the waves without hesitation.

Now, you might wonder how you can put a dog like that in a small cage for twenty-four hours. Answer: Give him one of Mom's Valiums, wrapped in a piece of cheese, just as he gets in the cage. The porter put the dog in the separate luggage car. On a few stops along the way, I got out and walked down to the luggage car to have look. Surf was stoned, mellow, and sleepy.

On the train ride, I read a story. Jesus was walking along the path with his disciples when they came upon a dead dog swarming with maggots. The disciples all turned away in total disgust. Jesus looked at the dog, turned to his disciples, and said, "His teeth are as white as pearls. There is a good thing in everything if you look deeply enough." I was touched by this attitude.

With no attraction to religion, I read the Bible and discovered that Jesus, unlike I had learned growing up, was not talking about a religion. He was talking about a way of living. He introduced a simple version of karma when he said, "You reap what you sow." He touched upon the wisdom of the scripture that tells us to seek the kingdom within us first, and all else shall be given." I was seeking internal answers, and I saw the "all else shall be given" as a good sign that I should continue to let the river carry me downstream.

Although the culture had not yet paved a clear path for these "esoteric" ways, a few magical writers and musicians spoke directly to the culture's needs and mine at the time. It was comforting to know that others had made their way and were kind enough to share and leave their mark.

Returning to Gainesville meant going home. By the time I got off the train and back to the trailer, I promised myself I would shut my mouth and not speak about the "oneness of everything" unless I was asked a direct question. Like trying to sit for meditation every day, I added keeping my mouth shut to my personal disciplines.

I found a job washing dishes at the local steak house, where I was quickly promoted to cooks' helper and then to steak cook for the Sunday morning, after-church crowd. It was a good job. It paid enough for me to live, with the added benefit that I could gather scraps of steak for the dogs.

It was the winter of 1974. The trailer had no heat until we converted a 55-gallon drum into a homemade woodstove. The single stovepipe caught the trailer on fire the first night, shortly after the stovepipe turned cherry-red. Luckily, the watering hose was nearby. Always it seemed that there was something to learn.

One Sunday after work, one of the waitresses and I spent some time together reading Be Here Now. A passage on page 39 in the brown pages referred to the male sex drive. It said, "You don't have to have that desire." After the army, I'd had that brief period of not having the desire, but it had passed. Now, I heard myself voice what for a twenty-one-year-old male to a female friend was the unthinkable: that I would like to try not to have that desire.

A few hours later, I was in her bedroom for the night. I told her, "No," and she got into bed naked, anyway. Apparently, she was willing to test my limit. I resisted touching and didn't sleep a wink all night from being overly aroused and refusing to give in. It was a test of my will power and discipline that wound up leaving me in severe pain, which is more commonly known as a bad case of blue balls.

And the point is? Well, I had gone from one extreme to the other. As I'd done after my first fast when I ate raw beets and cashews, I was trying something new without guidance and at my own risk in order to force a learning situation into motion.

Jeff had lived in Gainesville for over three years by then and had introduced me to some of his friends, but mostly we lived separate and opposite lives with different friends. I spent most of my time in the country, and he spent most of his time in town, getting involved with a consciousness-raising group called Arica that was run by a man named Oscar Ichazo.

In the two-and-a-half years since I had passed under the bridge and into the unknown, I had read and experienced enough to know that taking this river trip is not as easy as you might think when listening to the sales pitches of the different spiritual groups.

My good buddy Jeff and a friend of his named Joy were taking the Arica workshops and were trying to get me involved. However, from my observation, although there was no doubt that these people got high by whatever it was they were doing in class, I wondered whether they were calm and peaceful in their consciousness. It was my impression that their "high" was like a drug high. In fact, they got buzzed from practicing specific, esoteric breathing exercises for extended periods.

As I see it, the danger of repeating certain breathing techniques over and over in some zealous fashion can result in something similar to taking too much LSD and not being able to close the door once you come back. Psychic doors that are opened prematurely often force the personality into a more difficult fork in the river. And so, I have a golden rule: We must become "harmless" to ourselves, to the world, and to the people around us if we want to practice many of these esoteric methods safely. When I say safely, I mean that, like LSD, certain practices, when repeated over time and with intense focus, open the energy centers in the body, and if the personality/ego is not mature and grounded enough to handle the increased energy, it can get tossed out of its boat. Some people flip out on LSD, and some people flip out when they do advanced esoteric practices without preparation and for too long.

From my outside vantage point, it was easy to see that many of the public consciousness-raising schools and spiritual groups were extensions of much larger schools or groups in a major city. As a result, the founders sent out their students to teach the masses in smaller cities across the country. It was my opinion that all the schools made it sound too easy. Would a martial arts school start out a new white belt in a black-belt class? Of course not. But in those early days, it appeared that if you were willing to pay the fee, the school was willing to put you into advanced classes. Luckily, I had the good sense to know that I didn't need to practice breathing exercises while concentrating on opening up my energy centers. I knew for sure that I had already been unnaturally widened by the LSD.

For the majority of people, the curtain between the worlds is light-proof. When you take too much LSD or practice advanced esoteric methods, the curtain separating our worlds begins to allow light to seep through. It is called "enlightening" for a reason.

If I needed anything, it was a personal guide who understood where I was in my development, someone similar to a master in a martial arts' school who guides a student month after month and year after year. Why so long? How many years of devoted concentration does it take to become a master of the movement arts? Just to get to black belt, first degree, takes at least two years for a highly talented artist and three or more years for an average student. After that, you spend another year in training before you can test for the second-degree belt, two more years before you can test for the third-degree belt, an additional three years before fourth-degree, and so on until you reach the ninth-degree belt.

The point is: there are no shortcuts. I was getting a message that I should not be focusing on the light energy as a means of proving to my ego-self that I was consciously or spiritually high. In fact, I was getting the message that it was dangerous to do so.

Apart from this spiritual-light energy, new-age stuff, I spent many of my days near water. There was the little sinkhole I spoke about earlier, but there were other sinkholes, too. One was near Joy's house, which was within walking distance of our trailer. This sinkhole was several hundred feet long and maybe fifty-feet wide. The highest cliffs were approximately seventy-five feet high, and most of us could dive in headfirst. Another was an underground lake about a hundred feet by fifty feet, which was and thirty or forty feet down from the surface. There were two ways in. The obvious one was a fifteen- to twenty-foot diameter hole in the Earth, directly above the center of the lake. The other was a manhole-size opening at one edge of the underground lake. When you were in the water, looking up, most of what you saw was a ceiling made of Earth with a round opening to the sky. Off to one side, where the water ended, there was a way to climb up to the

Into the Unknown

Earth ceiling, and from there, maybe hundreds of years ago, someone dug an opening to the surface that was about the size of a manhole. Otherwise, if you had no rope, there would be no way out.

On occasion, we drove to the ocean, where we could park at the edge of a wild, sand-dune section of beach that extended for miles in either direction with no sight of a house or hotel.

These were the best of fun times, and it was during these trips that I met my friend, Doug. Doug and I dreamed up the idea of riding ten-speed bicycles from Gainesville to the 1974 World's Fair in Spokane Washington. To make this happen, I sold all of my possessions, including my stereo and album collection. The proceeds gave me enough cash to purchase a new, ten-speed bike with saddlebags, a sleeping bag, a rain tarp, and a one-man, mosquito-net tent that tied to trees (no poles). And I still had a few hundred dollars left for food.

Near the end of March, we started peddling north on a trip that would last two months.

During those days, we lived on fifteen dollars a week each. Mostly, we ate granola, peanut butter and jelly, and fruit. When we wanted something hot, we had brown lentils with carrots. We got our water from streams, rivers, and gas stations.

There were adventures, of course, but for me, it was a trip to settle me down. No drugs, meat, or beer. We traveled by bicycle for more than sixty days and camped anywhere we could. Early in the trip, we visited Doug's friend who lived on Sea Island, Georgia. There on the beach, we watched the full moon rise amid the crashing waves of high tide. After a long walk along the beach, we turned around. By then, the moon was so bright that we walked back through the sand dunes that ran parallel to the beach. If it had not been for the moonlight, we would never have considered doing that for fear of stepping on a cactus or a snake.

Perhaps ten feet into the sand dunes, I was struck by a cactus in my lower leg. It was weird, because I could swear I didn't brush into it. The moon was so bright that the sand glistened with reflection, and every living plant had a dark shadow as if it were in the shade line from the sun. And I was not staring at the sky as I walked; I was paying attention to where each next step landed. It happened to Doug, then again to me, except this time it was a bigger cactus, and it struck higher up on my leg. Again, I yelled. Now, I knew why these were called jumping cacti!

A day or two later, peddling our way north to Myrtle Beach, we were forced on to one of the major, two-lane highways heading north. There were too many trucks and cars for our comfort, so we stuck out our thumbs and hitched a ride in the back of a truck until we got past the heavy traffic.

It was our good luck to get picked up by a couple about our age who had been down in Florida, picking oranges. The oranges were a treat, and after driving for a while, we became friends. They offered to drive us to Myrtle Beach if we paid for the gas. We said, "Yes, of course!" Six bucks in those days could get you three hundred miles in a VW bus.

We stayed for only a day or two in Myrtle Beach and then peddled northwest to Fort Bragg, North Carolina, to visit Ray. From there, we would continue west and visit Doug's sister in Raleigh.

What was it like to visit Ray? I could swear that he wasn't the same guy, even though he was the same guy. It was as if my experience with Ray had been nothing to him. It seemed that he remembered very little of what he had told me was important to remember. Ray was the wise fellow who had guided me though the acid-light experience. What would have happened to me if he hadn't been there? How could he have been my guide and now have so little interest in it? I found it hard to believe. I have often wondered if another consciousness interfered in that experience. Was that possible?

The most memorable moment at Fort Bragg happened when we were walking down the sidewalk. A soldier walking past us seemed surprised to see two guys with longer than the normal army haircuts on the sidewalk. He looked at me with big, bright eyes and a smile and said, "What's happening?" I looked at him, and out of some bad habit, I responded by saying, "Nothing." I saw the light in his eyes go out. From that moment on, I have always tried to respond to that question with, "Everything,"

In Raleigh, we had our first real break. We stayed with Doug's sister, who had a home in a nice housing development. For the next few days, she took mercy upon us, fed us, and gave us nice beds and all the hot showers we wanted. I remember that we each got on the scale and were a little surprised at our new, low physical weight.

A few days later, we were off again, heading directly west into the North Carolina rolling hills, where we camped by streams. When possible, we visited college campuses to take showers in the men's locker rooms and enjoy a change of scenery.

At one such school, we met a female student who asked Doug and me to hitchhike to the Kentucky Derby with her. Why not? So, we parked our bikes in her dorm room and hitched enough rides to get us there and back in relative ease. It was an interesting and enjoyable adventure for the three of us. She was like a sister, and when we did sleep, she lay between us for protection. I don't remember much about the Derby except that it was crowded on the infield and we could only briefly see the horses as they passed. The highlight was when someone climbed the flagpole in the center of the racetrack and pulled his pants down to the roar of fifty thousand fans. Back in 1974, it was called "streaking."

Hitchhiking "home" late in the day after the Derby, we were picked up by someone who turned out to be a needle-shooting, nice-guy druggie. We didn't know that when we accepted the invitation to spend the night at his apartment. But soon after we got there and found our spots on the floor in a back room, the party started. Not once did anyone bother us, but for hours and hours, we listened to the very loud party of happy junkies getting fucked up. In the morning, he drove us out to the road we needed to be on to get back to the college.

Doug and I continued on our way. The riding was becoming increasingly difficult as the hills of western North Carolina turned into mountains. Even though we were both in good physical shape, we finally gave up and stuck out our thumbs. Several hours later, we were riding our bikes through the city Boone.

Boone is a university town high in mountains where we once again found it easy to meet people and hang out for a few days. On the morning we planned to leave, a friend suggested that he drive us to the top of the mountain pass. From there, he said, it was all downhill into Tennessee. In fact, we coasted downhill all day and then made our way towards Knoxville, where I had the address of a few friends (girls) I had met on the beach during the summer of 1973.

As we rode into Tennessee, we discussed the possibility of inviting girlfriends to join us on the trip. At the time, I did not have a girlfriend, but I invited Marilyn, whom I had known since sixth grade. It was a wild guess, and it didn't work out. Doug had a girlfriend he had been dating when we left for the World's Fair, and she was happy to accept his invitation.

We had been on the road for six weeks and had reached a nice lake where we could camp out on the outskirts of the Knoxville area while we waited for Lynn to gather her things and arrive at the Greyhound bus station near us. In the meantime, I made contact with friends from Myrtle Beach, and one of their parents drove to the lake, picked Doug and me up, and took us to their home for dinner. I remember the mother not being impressed, or I should say that she was slightly appalled, when Doug told her that his girlfriend would be joining us on the bike trip in the next few days.

We were still camping at the lake outside of Knoxville when Lynn got off the bus with her bike. It was nice to see that she and Doug were so happy. The next morning, we set out riding west. A few days later, we were camped out in a thick forest when it started to rain and kept raining all day. All those hours alone in my tent got me thinking and feeling that it was time for a change.

On the bike trip, we carried two books: Be Here Now and the I Ching. The I Ching is similar to Tarot or animal cards in that the questioner tosses coins or pulls a card or series of cards for a reading. The results can be uncanny if you are serious and clear in your intention as you hold a question in your mind. This rainy day in the tent, I tossed the I Ching coins. The result spoke directly to my question. It said that it was time to end my trip and go back to Jersey for the summer. And so, I did. A little over two months from when I had started the trip, I packed up my bike at some bus station in Tennessee and moved back into my parents' naturally cool basement.

That summer, for money, I road my bike to the exclusive Jewish Green Brook Country Club and carried two big golf bags eighteen holes for eighteen dollars cash. It was a nice, easy summer, and by early September, I was back in Florida.

To earn some money, I returned to the steak restaurant. By then, Jeff and I had gone in completely different directions. He was completely involved in a consciousness-raising group, and I was still busy trying to discipline myself to sit and meditate every day and read more books. By then, Castaneda had written two more books, The Separate Reality and The Journey to Exelon. I also read other helpful books, such as Jonathan Livingston Seagull, by Richard Bach.

That Christmas of 1974 found me back in Jersey for the holidays and to attend the wedding of a friend toward the end of January. I was also in need of cash, so I applied to be an usher at the local movie theater in Totowa. I got to hold a flashlight and help seat the nine hundred people who would pack the theater on a Friday or Saturday night. The movie playing at the time was the world premiere of Earthquake. The big deal with that movie was the special speaker system placed in the theater that literally shook the building and the people in it. Later in the year, when the movie was released to other cities across the country, some theaters had problems with plaster and such falling off the walls and ceilings. We did not have that problem. As ushers, we watched this movie at least five times a week for months and were able to pick out all the fake disaster scenes.

It was a real treat in the spring when the Who's movie Tommy came to our theater. It attracted huge, happy crowds on the weekends. That was when I met Pat and Brian and Pat's little sister, Kathi, who would later become my wife. We were married on August 24, 1975, by a minister friend at his church in West Paterson, not by a priest in the Catholic Church, which was the religion of both our families.

I mention the "two-church" story only because, within a week of our wedding, a woman wrote in to the opinion column of the local newspapers, saying something like, "How could two Catholic families with the last names O'Brian and Carroll let their kids get married at a Methodist Church?" She was quite simply appalled. The times were changing.

In fact, Kathi and I did visit a Catholic priest to discuss our marriage plans, and he refused to marry us because Kathi was only seventeen, though almost eighteen. For wedding gifts, we received money and camping gear. As I remember, we netted $2,100 and were 100 percent debt-free. We packed the blue 1963 Chevy Impala that I received from Scott Spencer. We were going to Taos, New Mexico, where we would meet the guru, Herman Rednick.

Chapter 7:
HERMAN AND TAOS

We left New Jersey with my friend Doug in the car. He had hitched a ride from Gainesville to be at our wedding, so Kathi and I were driving him to his parent's house in North Carolina. From there, we turned the car west and drove straight to my friend Robert's house. Robert had visited Jeff and me in Gainesville, and I had gone to his wedding in January. Robert and his wife, Joan, now lived in a cabin in a remote mountain area east of Albuquerque.

Robert had met Herman back in 1973, when he moved to Taos for a short while. Through Robert's connections, we met Charles and Maria, who led a meditation class for us at their home using Herman's teachings as a simple introduction and preparation for meeting Herman later that afternoon.

The word guru is used to refer to a conscious being who helps guide an individual's personality to their own true soul. A genuine guru is not looking for followers or money. He has his own methods, and to become a disciple, you must agree to do the work he requires and then follow through by actually practicing the prescribed discipline year in and year out.

The Guru

During the half hour ride south to Taos to meet Herman, once again I encountered an internal crisis: very tight canyon walls and Class 4 rapids. I feared a big let down if things didn't go well with Herman. Would I get tossed out of my boat?

Herman was seventy-three years old when we met. Upon arrival, we were offered instant coffee or tea and a graham cracker on a small plate. Soon, we entered Herman's studio. The walls were covered with oil paintings of the spiritual realm done in vibrant colors. A section of the studio was devoted to comfortable chairs where a few disciples and visitors could meet with Herman to discuss personal and spiritual issues.

By then, I was four years downriver from the bridge of my childhood. I hoped this guy Herman was the real deal. I knew I could use a little personal spiritual guidance.

When it was my turn to speak, I told my story about the mescaline trip in Florida, the army, and the LSD trip on the beach with Ray. When I finished, he looked at me and said, "We will do it the natural way."

A wave of calm, pure love washed over my being. I had braved the rapids and made it home. Finally, I could unbuckle my life vest and float on the river with no fear of being capsized.

When Herman referred to the "natural way," he meant we would do it through purification of body and mind. With his guidance, I would build a stable foundation based on a clear understanding of the two voices we all carry in our heads. Those voices represent the two parts of the Self. The first is the ego personality, and the second is the soul. Herman taught that our true purpose as humans was to transmute our personality into a clear channel for the light and love of the Christ while we are living and working in a physical body in the world.

There was no excuse for wishing injury upon another person or for holding on to resentment on any level. We learned that these types of mental and emotional thoughts and feelings were dense, heavier than thoughts and feelings of love and kindness. If we wanted to rise up in consciousness, we would have to train our minds how to recognize and purge the heavy ideas that bring us down and try to keep us there.

Herman's teaching purposely focused on doing this yogic practice during the normal forty-hour work week and at home within our closest relationships.

In essence, we were learning about our internal behavior and how it relates to the main purpose of our life. If we believe that our purpose is to love everyone and take the advice of Jesus when he told us to love our enemies, then how do we deal with the people who annoy us or piss us off? How deep do they get under our skin and affect the way we think and feel? Do they make us boil? Are they really a threat to our health and well-being, or are we just playing out an annoying or painful drama over and over in our heads?

In times like these, the ego personality usually needs to take a chill pill, a time-out, or a walk in the woods to engage in a conversation between the two inner voices. If the ego is smart, it will learn to listen to the soul; and if the ego is foolish it will ignore the soul's voice and seek revenge or hold on to resentments, simply because it feels offended.

Even when everything is crazy, the soul remains unaffected. Like a teacher observing a child, it watches, knowing all the time that the child is still deeply involved in a learning process. From a spiritual perspective, the more intense situations we encounter provide opportunities to learn how to navigate difficult times. We can either become afraid and angry and hold on to resentment as we ride the turbulent waters, or, with trust and concentration, we can ride joyfully like kids keeping their balance on a 55-gallon-drum raft during a flood.

Transmuting the Personality

How do we transmute the personality into a vehicle for the soul? What kind of disciplined practice do we need to follow within our Self to get to the place where we see our reactions to all daily experiences through both the light of the soul's consciousness and the awareness of the personality? If we want soul presence on Earth, we need to clear out the toxins in our bodies and minds that block the light and the finer quality of our vibrations. When I say vibrations, I am referring to vibrating energy. Everything is made up of vibrating energy, and we were seeking what we might call a cleaner, purer, more spiritually attuned vibration.

We have to remember that our soul is where we find our Self when this life passes. Our soul is present, always watching over our ego personality as it goes through its daily drama. The brightness of a soul is easy to see and feel in the presence of a young child, but often it fades into the background as the ego personality learns to survive in the world and forgets about the inner journey in which we are also involved.

We live in a less than nurturing world where fear, resentment, and junk food pollute our mass consciousness. We don't have to hold on to these destructive habits, thoughts, and feelings, but often we do. They are like weeds in a garden. We can pull them out or let them take over. It is no different with thoughts. We need to develop awareness of what we are thinking, feeling, and imagining. The soul is willing to shine the light if the personality is willing to open its eyes and get out of the way. Either way, we still have to live and work in this world.

With Herman, we were learning how to keep our balance as we maneuvered through the inner-life river canyons of being young married with kids while working. At the age we were, everyone's boat capsizes. No one gets through those rough, challenging years without getting dunked in the cold, turbulent waters numerous times.

If the ego gets hurt and bruised, it can choose to hold on to the pain or let it go. When you train the personality to be grateful for every experience, no matter how difficult, that makes it easier to climb back in your boat and continue downstream. Resentment makes life difficult and assures us that we will have to repeat difficult experiences until we figure out why we should be grateful—and then actually be grateful all the way through the difficult experience. One approach brings calm and clarity; the other brings turbulence. And our response in the present creates our future situation on the river.

Our guru had a following of thirty to fifty active disciples from a wide range of backgrounds and professions. Together, we shared the experience of Sunday morning class. Always, we sat quietly and breathed consciously and rhythmically. We would breathe in for seven counts, hold for three, breathe out for seven, hold for three, and then repeat. A beginner might do only three breaths in and three out with one hold. Rhythmic breath brings awareness to our breathing pattern. Are we chest-breathing or belly-breathing? To breathe deeply and slowly, we need to avoid expanding and contracting our chest and instead breathe in and out with our belly. A good test to see how you are breathing is to lie on the floor with something on your belly, such as a small, flat stone or a book, and observe how your breath moves the object. If you are breathing with your belly, the object should be clearly rising and lowering with each breath. The slower and more deeply we can breathe, the calmer our mind and body can become.

For meditation, we want to belly breathe. We want our physical body to relax enough to feel comfortable as it sits quietly for the duration of the meditation. In the beginning, we may only be able to sit and breathe for five minutes before we can no longer resist the urge to get up and go about our daily activities.

Once you are comfortable with sitting and breathing, you can extend the practice to include a mantra. A mantra can be many things, but in essence, it is a sound or phrase that you repeat over and over to help you calm the waters of a noisy mind and body. "Om" is a universal mantra that anyone can use. You chant, extending the Om syllable for the duration of your out breath.

Meditating with a mantra for the first time could make you feel like a teacher entering a classroom full of noisy kids who have never learned to sit quietly in their seats. Wild thoughts can easily overpower your attention, just as loud music can overpower your ability to hear anything else.

Softly, on those Sundays, we chanted out loud the sound "Ooommmmmm" on each out breath for a minute or two and then slowly turned the sound inward until we were no longer speaking it with our breath, but saying it silently from within.

In a matter of seconds, you will notice that your thoughts will start wandering away from the Om and thinking about work or the kids or whatever else might be on your mind. With intent, you will keep remembering that you are meditating and are supposed to be repeating Om, and then Om again.

This is a good, safe place to start. If you practice every day, as we did, gradually the five minutes will expand to ten and then fifteen, and eventually it will settle at twenty or more minutes.

Practicing as a group, our rhythmic breathing and chanting calmed our individual and group waters. This was not getting us high like the group experience I had in Gainesville. In Taos, our intended purpose was to calm the body and our thinking mind so that the energy of love, light, and wisdom could pour though our hearts and minds and into the world unobstructed.

Each week Herman gave us a lesson to ponder and to meditate upon, using the mantra that accompanied the lesson. For homework, we were required to write a short paper pertaining to lessons learned or the experiences we had over the week. It was to be no more than a few, short paragraphs which we read in class on the following Sunday, one by one, after the group chant.

After listening to everyone read, the group came full circle for the week. Herman slowly read the new lesson and mantra for everyone to write down. He answered questions and one of the disciples sang a beautiful song. Class over, we were sent back into the world of human relationships for another week to practice our yoga.

The original meaning of yoga is union. The union is with the oneness of spirit. There are many pathways to union with our spirit. One kind is hatha yoga, which is the physical, meditative practice of stretching poses. There is also devotional yoga, known as bhakti yoga; raja yoga, or union through the mind, and what is called the yoga of "the beloved," in which we find union within a relationship. In the Seventies, and particularly within Herman's group, all spiritual work was considered "our yoga."

The suggested time for daily, personal meditation, which sets our tone and intention for the day, was between four and five a.m. We did not dread going to work, because no matter what happened, we were practicing our yoga. We were becoming aware that gratitude for every experience was an important and necessary component to clearing the inner channel. It's the ego/personality that creates all the problems. If we are not happy about something, becoming resentful only makes it worse. Justifiable resentment opens the door to the toxins of hate and fear that lower our vibration.

We were learning that the key to gaining access to higher dimensions of consciousness within our Self was accessible only if we purified our thinking minds and opened our hearts enough to let the love and wisdom of the universe flow through. Once I said to Herman, "I want to have a calm mind and an open heart." He looked at me and said, "A calm mind and an open and loving heart."

When we pour out our personal love, we get drained if we are not loved in return. But higher love, the love that comes from God or the Great Spirit, is eternal, and it is never draining.

Herman was teaching that our spiritual work (yoga) was to be practiced during our professional careers, during our daily life interactions, and within our personal relationships. Daily meditation, the use of a mantra all day, and eliminating alcohol, drugs (such as weed, etc.), and meat were all part of the training.

Many of the students had the opportunity to visit privately with Herman in his studio once a week. My day was Saturday because I worked Monday through Friday. Always I enjoyed these visits. These were the intimate times when disciples could ask deep personal and spiritual questions. These were the moments when we could fine-tune our understanding of the way it all works. These were the moments and days of great love and vulnerability.

Disillusionment

I mentioned the yoga of "the beloved." A basic part of Herman's teaching included the understanding and practice of "the beloved" yoga. The essence of this yoga is to seek the divine in our partner and learn to love unconditionally, especially when the boat you are both in encounters a rocky patch. This beautiful yoga was taught by Herman and practiced by everyone in the group.

Thus, it came as a huge surprise when it was revealed that Herman had been playing around with a few of the disciples' wives over the years! Most of us learned about the scandal one Sunday morning. One of Herman's oldest and most devoted disciples stood up in class and read a paper that stated, "The sacred trust between Herman and me has been broken," and then walked out without saying another word.

Our canyon walls contracted when it became obvious that things were not exactly the way many of us disciples had assumed. How could Herman play around with the young wives while teaching this yoga? Most of us had assumed Herman was celibate, but had anyone ever asked or raised the question? Not that I remember.

For most, if not all, there was no way out of this river canyon, and the current had sped up. There were no areas where we could pull over and camp for the night. Ahead, we could hear the thunderous sound of the river pouring over the falls.

Within weeks, the group that had been together for over ten years went over the falls and split in two. One side defended Herman, and the other side was angry and pissed and left the group. When I finally regained my senses, I found myself split in two. I was angry with my teacher for hiding his actions because I had assumed he was perfect. I was blown away that Herman had intimate affairs with female disciples behind the backs of their disciple husbands. It seemed to me that my friend, the old disciple, had had hot coals dropped in his lap, and some people were judging him because he was crying out in his anger and pain. I was in shock.

I confronted Herman on my next Saturday visit and was told a few days later by his inner circle not to come back on Saturdays. That was fine. I was upset, but I still went to class every Sunday. On weekdays, when our wives and children were still asleep, my friend Charles Dillon and I would walk to the meditation building at four in the morning for meditation, as we had before. We would return by six, just in time to feed the kids and get off to work. On Sundays, Charles and I always went early to start the fire in the woodstove in the meditation building. Depending on the time of year, we could have an hour or two in silence before other group members started to arrive.

Because we were the fire keepers, Charles and I always had the best, front-row seats for class. However, after this ordeal of trust, I moved my seat back a few rows. It's hard not to be critical when the shit hits the fan. Certain people in the group drove me crazy internally. Their blind obedience without question and the way they looked at Herman with goo-goo eyes rocked my boat. The calm, meditative state I'd experienced from the two hours of early meditation would evaporate. I couldn't believe some of the questions I was hearing. One guy offered up his wife to sleep with Herman because he had heard that if she slept with the guru, she would get some of the guru's vibration, and then he, the husband, will get some of that vibration from his wife! My mind flipped out in judgment on this guy. There were other crazy questions during these turbulent times. I found it best to keep my mouth shut and try to simply observe while doing my best to love everyone without criticism.

Here is a little perspective on the situation. Some time in the late 1970s, Herman moved from his house and studio in Taos to the Lorain community north of Questa. In Lorain, his house was built next to and shared a courtyard with the elder disciple who had spilled the beans in class. It was then 1983, and because of that upset, Herman had to move. Luckily, another disciple in the neighborhood offered Herman a piece of land next to his house, and he had footed the bill for building a new house.

This was a great opportunity for me, because I became the licensed general contractor with a crew of disciples. We got the job to build Herman's new house. The house was a total pleasure to build, and by the time it was completed, the better part of a year or more had passed since the scandal. By the time Herman moved into his new house over a year later, much of the drama in my head had settled, while for others it was just beginning. One of my friends had a wife who wanted to sleep with Herman. She came to my friend and asked for permission to spend the night in Herman's bed. I remember my friend struggling with the desire to somehow justify it. Somewhere inside his mind, he was looking for a way to bless the request of his wife, but he just couldn't do it. Emotionally, it didn't work. It didn't feel good to him. His relationship ended along with those of a few others whose wives wanted to spend more time with Herman.

It was my good friend, David, who told me, "Don't throw the baby out with the bath water." That simple statement hit directly home.

The drama around the scandal had very little to do with my personal life. My wife wasn't sleeping with the guru, nor did she want to sleep with him.

The range of the reactions to Herman's behavior was wide. The old disciple who'd had hot coals dropped in his lap and spilled the beans was on the extreme end of the range; others refused to let go of their resentment for feeling or thinking they had been betrayed, and yet other disciples followed him without question.

After much soul searching, I came to the conclusion that Herman had not betrayed me. His teachings and guidance had been impeccable in my personal relationship with him. Who was I to judge what lesson a person needs in order to move on to the next level of consciousness?

The following Sunday I reclaimed my front row seat and requested a visit in his studio. I had survived the wild ride through the tight canyon. I confessed to Herman that it was too difficult to maintain my practice of getting up at four a.m. for meditation while working as a full-time carpenter, running a construction company, and taking care of the needs of a family of four at home. He looked at me and said, "Your work is now your yoga." It had been a relentless process for me to work through all my issues with Herman and resolve the judgments I held toward my brothers and sisters, but the waters were once again calm and clear.

The Guru Crosses the Rainbow Bridge

The expression "crossing the rainbow bridge" is a reference to the event of dying. When it was Herman's time to die, he called a few close disciples to sit in meditation with him while he went through the process. I wasn't there, but soon after Herman's crossing, my friend, Charles, called to tell me that something special was happening and suggested I come. I called my friend, David, who some years earlier had suggested that I not throw the baby out with the bathwater when it came to the imperfections of Herman the physical personality and the teachings he was transmitting. Together we drove over to Herman's house. When I entered the room where his body lay, my consciousness was instantly altered. I entered into a profound state of calm, meditative bliss!

Following are a few short papers I wrote for class that I wish to share.

At thirty-one, I am still a child. Patience I must have. I cannot say what my spiritual work will be tomorrow, but today I know it is in the busyness of my daily life. I extend a hand to a brother in the marketplace as a wave of divine love pours over us.

How far will living these truths take me? I feel like I'm just beginning, yet I'm already too far along to turn back. So here I am. I must transmute my nature and clear this personality of everything that hinders my walking the spiritual path; I must find my blocks and dissolve them with Love and Will. How else can I stop the negative thoughts and emotions from entering and blocking the flow between my soul and this physical form?

• • •

Where else could I find the brotherhood but within my heart? I focus on Christ and remember to touch a brother with love.

My thinking mind is finding a brotherhood with my heart and my heart is discovering the unity of brotherhood in everyone I meet. I am grateful for the guidance of those in the unseen worlds.

• • •

Destiny provides the opportunity but I choose what to do.

Freedom is around us at every moment if we would be clear enough to see it. The mysteries unfold along the way.

I opened the book "The Way of the White Clouds" and read, "Every human personality has shortcomings, and as long as we are engaged in observing the imperfections of others we deprive ourselves of the opportunities of learning from them. Remember that every being carries within itself the spark of Buddha-hood, but as long as we concentrate on other peoples' faults we deprive ourselves of the light that in degrees shines out from our fellow beings." These few lines broke a hypnotic hold on me for I do engage in seeing faults in some people, and surely, I've missed seeing God when the presence was there. I am told to Love, because by doing so, my brother becomes my teacher, my sister becomes the light on my path. This form can become a channel to help others find their way.

• • •

I am here to serve, not to spend time focusing on psychic phenomenon. I am here to love, not to try to develop energy centers before their time. Herman told me that if I open my heart in service and love, the other centers will open naturally. I am grateful for this guidance. I used to think, "I want psychic experiences to let me know I am growing spiritually." But now, through guidance on the Christ Path, I can see my growth through my reactions to different experiences. When I go through a difficult experience, remain loving, and have understanding and compassion for those around me, I have made a step toward the city of God. As I love, the spiritual world will unfold before me as the world unfolds before a child.

• • •

I must transmute the personality so that every breath of my life becomes the reality of light and love. It is not a thing to be turned on or off in different situations. It is the point of fire, the intense focus toward the divine that will bring me through the illusion into reality. In a world of a billion distractions, I need help.

I was given the vision to see an old pattern of coldness I had toward my brother in a recurring situation. This week, I will love him. This week, I will speak truth when it needs to be spoken.

Everyone is my brother, and in my heart and mind, I know this is true.

Chapter 8:
TIME TO REST, ASSIMILATE, AND PLAY

When Herman died, I was thirty-three, still a young man. My life was going full tilt. I had a wife, three daughters, and a construction company. By then, I also had a good eleven years of meditation under my belt. My wild mind with its racing thoughts had calmed to a degree, but I recognized that I still needed more relaxation.

Taking time off from work regularly is not acceptable in this culture, yet I had learned early in my life the importance of taking breaks. It presented a dilemma. Fortunately, I was lucky enough to land next to a disciple named Roy when the group shit about Herman hit the fan and many of us plunged over the waterfall. Roy was a dentist who always took Wednesday afternoons off. It was natural for me to do the same, and so we started playing golf every week.

Talking without Talking

While driving to and from the nearest golf course, which was up in the mountains, we verbally processed our thoughts and feelings about what had taken place in the group. Often, when Roy and I got in the car, we'd start talking in such a deep, focused way that by the time we arrived at the golf course, we didn't remembered driving through the towns along the way.

For a full eight years, we had been floating along on a beautiful, safe, and enchanting stretch of river, never expecting or considering that something terrible might happen, when, abruptly, the current sped up, signaling a rapid change, and my raft was swept over a hundred-foot waterfall. Smash. Crash. Out cold. By the time I had regained some form of consciousness, my world had completely changed. Everything I had been relying on outside myself had lost its value. Yet, the tonal world, the physical, remained the same: work, little kids, a partner, and the four seasons. How do you describe the impact of something so extremely disorienting when you have never experienced anything like it before?

Such was the shift I experienced when it was time to leave Herman's nest and do life on my own. Herman had become a huge, calming, loving, and guiding force that many had come to rely on. Then came the day when it was time to take charge of the oars as if my life depended on it. No longer could I rely on the safety of my teacher's guidance. And yet, from my perspective, the break-up of the Herman group was a beautiful gift. It was a great lesson, and the final exam had to do with always being grateful while loving everyone we meet and everyone who enters our thoughts. If we could do that, then who is to judge the final lesson? It was perfect. Everyone got exactly what they needed so as to move on to the next level of walking the path of love and service.

The bottom of the waterfall was not a pretty sight, and yet, the river continued on. I had so much internal confusion going on after plunging over the falls that I was struggling almost to the point of exhaustion. That was when my brother, David, advised, "Don't throw the baby out with the bathwater."

I know, we've all heard that a million times, but on that one day, suddenly, as if I had put on a magic pair of glasses, I could see through the murk and tell the difference between the baby and the bathwater.

One day, after more than ten years of perfectly clean living with no weed or beer, Roy and I went on a mountain stream hike that was on the way to the Taos Ski Valley. We had walked maybe a few hundred feet on a single-file path along the small stream when Roy broke out a joint of some really good weed. Together, after all those years of daily meditation, practice, and clean living, we sat down and passed that joint back and forth. We got so high that we started communicating our thoughts without speaking. This continued on and off for hours before we had a thought about our lives in the physical world. We had to keep reminding each other of the daily physical life that awaited us. We had wives, kids, and businesses. It was another few hours before we were ready to drive back into the world.

The Swift Currents of the Harmonic Convergence

That "talking without talking" experience marked a time of much healing and recovery. By a strange coincidence, the Harmonic Convergence in August of 1987 was a time of major change that marked our entrance as a planet into the photon band. To explain, Earth travels around the sun in 365 days, and the sun also has an orbit that it follows, along with all its planets. Now, visualize the shape of a racetrack. Imagine that you are driving along the straightaway section at 69,000 miles per hour as you begin to enter the curve. That moment of entering the celestial curve was given the name "The Harmonic Convergence."

I know that some have had the feeling that life has been speeding up, and this curve could be one of the reasons. All drivers know the feeling of entering a curve at 60 mph. This is the same, but on a vast scale. The curve is also called the photon band, the New Age, the Age of Aquarius, or as we learned in 2012, the time after the end of the Mayan calendar. All of these names refer to the new atmosphere of light that is permeating Earth reality and will continue to do so for the next two thousand years. On a huge scale, we can think of it in terms of night and day, where the nights are the long straightaway that lasts eleven thousand years, and the daylight is the curve, which lasts for two thousand years before heading again back into the night. It's a 26,000-year cycle that also coincides with the complete cycle of our twelve zodiac signs.

The cycle of the Herman days from Gainesville to the Convergence had come to completion for us as a family, and the need to work to support the household took main stage.

Mother Nature Heals

A few weeks later, for the long Labor Day weekend, Rick, my friend and plumbing contractor during those years, decided to rent a motorboat and take our families camping at Navajo Lake for the last weekend of the summer. We had so much fun fishing and boating with our families that Rick and I soon went in fifty-fifty on a good used boat that could safely handle four adults and our five little kids. Our families camped every other weekend starting from Memorial Day and ending on Labor Day. In between those two summer holidays, we left Taos after lunch on Thursdays and did not return until sundown on Sunday.

In those days, the traffic light at the north end of Taos was a single, blinking light. That light marked the crossroads of the Ski Valley, the Gorge Bridge, the town of Taos, and north to Questa and Colorado. These were the days before cell phones. We didn't hear the messages on our tape machines until either late Sunday or early Monday morning.

I had an internal rule: Once I turned left at the blinking light and drove toward Gorge Bridge and on to Navajo Lake, I would no longer allow myself to think or talk about work. It was time to play with family and go fishing. The one other factor I truly loved was how enjoyable the kids were when we were camping. By the time they woke up Friday morning, the chill pill of Mother Nature had taken effect. The cranky bickering you might expect with five or six kids, and sometimes a few more, depending on the weekend, simply vanished. It was as close to heaven on Earth as I could imagine with a family of kids.

While summer camping with the family, Rick and I always got up at dawn to go fishing while everyone else was still asleep. We would return in time for Rick to cook breakfast for the kids while I took care of the boat and the ladies packed lunches into the coolers.

When the kids were fed, we loaded everyone into the boat and went looking for a remote place along the hundred and sixty miles of coastline to set up the base camp for the day. A workable campsite needed a few things: a beach to tie up the boat, cliffs for the kids to jump off of, good rocks for the kids to fish off of, and a place for everyone to sit. Once all the coolers and extra people were unloaded at the base camp, it was usually my time to start waterskiing and tubing all the kids and adults who were interested.

After that, we'd park the boat back at the day camp where the kids could dive off of rocks, fish, and eat lunch. When all the kids were tired out, we'd load up and go back to the main camp. It was then, because the kids were so mellow, nice, and easy, that we boys were freed of our fatherly duties to go fishing again for a few hours before dinnertime.

Mother Nature heals. Spending time in nature is the natural way to get and keep our energy centers clean and healthy. No one would argue that Mother Nature heals. The trick is to figure out how to get enough of "Her" to heal in the first place and then to maintain that level as we continue to live our daily lives out in the world. When it comes to physical exercise, many say that we need to exercise three times a week for six months before we can finally say, "I am in good shape." So, how often do we need to take a break from our busy daily lives in order to maintain our mental and emotional health? Are two weeks, weekends, and a few long holiday weekends a year enough?

Yes, I was my own boss and could do what I wanted. But it was not that simple. It takes discipline to do what is necessary to ensure that everyone is happy when we are gone, and also happy when we return. Many fellow contractors told me they wished they could take more time off from their businesses, but they never felt secure enough to do it. I was told the same story by certain soldiers at Fort Jackson when they told me that they wished they had the balls to do what I was doing.

Okay, so I am a little weird—but not that weird.

Taking ample time off felt so good and right that I often preached to my friends the belief that you can actually accomplish more in your business when you learn to take time off regularly. What I mean by regular is a four- or five-day healthy getaway at least four times a year to do something that you love so that when you return, you are refreshed and more balanced than before you left. If you don't come back refreshed, then your time off doesn't count as healthy.

Saying that you can't take time off or make time during the day or week is the same as saying you can't quit smoking." Sure, you can, but you have to want it badly enough that you actually do something to alter your present course.

Take Time to Play Canyon

To make a change in our life, we need to be looking for a fork in the river. Sometimes, the forks are huge and visible from a distance as they divide the one river into two clear choices; and sometimes, they appear as side forks that you come upon unexpectedly. My best friends and I took the fork without hesitation whenever we saw the sign: Take Time to Play Canyon.

Take Time to Play is a magical canyon, because it allows us time to be free of the physical, mental, and emotional stress associated with living and working in the modern, workaday world so we can begin the healing process. Now, choosing how much time to spend in this canyon is a delicate balance.

Having a 115-horsepower boat naturally opened the door to remote-lake camping and fishing trips in the off-season with my friends Rick and Bernie. It didn't take long for us to establish seasonal trips: end of September fishing trip and Super Bowl weekend fly-fishing trips on the San Juan; the April joint birthday trip to Concha Lake/Lake Powell to celebrate Bernie and me; and the company camping/fishing tourney in late June or early July. There were other trips of course, without the family, but these were considered holidays or necessary in order to help maintain some form of balance in normal daily life.

The delicate balance had to do with how many days could we get away with taking between our business and family obligations without rocking anyone's boat. We started with the summer family camping trips and four or more four- to five-day camping trips with just the boys. As the years passed, we added more days.

To play like this as an adult with a job and a family, a minimum of two things are required. One, figure out how to take more time off from work without causing difficulties there and, two, if you are going to have fun while your other half stays home with the kids, be sure to get your spouse's blessing to be away and have a good time.

Resentment boils if those two things are not working in your favor. Many fathers of kids hear comments like, "While you're out having a good time, I'm home dealing with the kids," so it's a fine line to walk. I've been accused of playing too much, which I think sounds like getting yelled at for coming home all wet and full of mud after building rock and mud dams down at the brook. It's all about finding the right balance. We need to learn to recognize the imbalance and take corrective measures.

This need for play includes the moms, as well. Parents in general need a life outside of family and work, and in my mind, there is no doubt that "play" is the gateway to all art forms and a more balanced life.

In addition to play, we also need to pay attention to our physical bodies and our emotions. As a carpenter who built houses, I had to keep learning new ways to keep my lower back healthy. Chiropractic, energy work, and deep-tissue body work became a way of life. If a doctor or practitioner moved away or no longer "felt right," I sought another.

Rebirthing

During one of my seeking periods, Dr. Terry Rudd, NA, moved into the office next to my bookkeeper. I made an appointment to see what he had to offer. We talked for an hour. He suggested four "rebirthing" sessions, once a week for a month. Although I never heard of rebirthing, I decided it would be worth a try. Rebirthing, in my experience, is a technique for uncovering old wounds that were covered up internally before they were allowed or given the opportunity to be properly healed.

Terry instructed me on how to breathe while sitting comfortably on the floor with pillows. You begin by pulling the breath in through the nose, just as an archer pulls back an arrow in a bow, and then letting the breath out through the mouth fast, as if letting the arrow fly. In and out; in and out. Terry gently reminded me to breathe in this manner for five minutes or maybe fifteen minutes. I repeatedly pulled the bow and released the arrow until, unexpectedly, I found myself in the basement of my parents' house during the Christmas holiday season of 1957. I was five, and my brothers were eleven, thirteen, and fifteen years old. They had just carried all the boxes of Christmas decorations down from the attic and had begun to unpack them and decorate the basement. Our parents had nothing to do with it. Dennis, my oldest brother and the artist of the family, with the help of Tommy and Walter, turned the basement into a Christmas wonderland that included a train set, villages, and all the trimmings. Decorating the basement usually started the Friday after Thanksgiving. It was always a blissful, colorful time of year. Later, I realized that this first session had been an uncommonly gentle introduction to rebirthing.

The second rebirthing session wasn't as gentle or pleasant as the first. I breathed, pulling the bow and releasing the arrow, and all of a sudden, I was fourteen months old and playing under my family's kitchen table. I was walking from one chair to another, staying out of the way while the party guests were busy clearing the dinner plates and getting ready for dessert and coffee. It was then that I noticed a rope dangling from the counter and ventured out across the room to grab hold. As I was holding on with my left hand, I grabbed with my right and pulled a little harder for support, only to be greeted with a blast of blinding pain. This was no rope. It was the cord to the percolator! The coffee poured over my head and shoulders as I screamed. The pain, blinding as it was, only lasted a few moments until the angels came and took me out of my body. There was no way to cope with or understand what had just happened, and I suspect this is why the angels were present. In the hospital, I lay covered from head to toe in gauze while everyone wondered if I would live or die. Then the pain returned. I was crying—no, I was bawling uncontrollably on the pillows when I realized it was not my pain I was feeling but my mother's! It was very sad, because I was okay, yet my mother was overwhelmed with guilt. In this second session, I was able to see, feel, and understand that my mother didn't handle the burn situation very well and tumbled into depression from the guilt.

I found rebirthing a valuable tool for healing. Over the years, I participated in several rebirthing workshops and training sessions where we paired up with another person so we could practice being the guide, just as Terry was being a guide for me. The main purpose of the guide is to hold the sacred space for this very intimate experience and give assistance when needed for physical comfort, as people eventually ended up on mats with a blanket and some pillows.

I must have held the space as a guide for twenty-five rebirthing sessions over time, and although I am sure I guided a male a time or two, my memory brings forth only women. In general, men did not go to workshops like this, and not one of my male friends showed any interest in experiencing the rebirthing process. From what I saw and felt, most sessions gave rise to the difficulties women had experienced living in a female body while growing up. It seemed to me that all of those sessions involved some form of physical, emotional, mental, or sexual abuse.

Revisiting Past Wounds

After the initial Christmas wonderland experience, several sessions in succession revisited past wounds that had to be witnessed and healed before the pulling of the bow and letting the arrow fly no longer took me into painful past experiences. The breathing seemed to function like a military mine-sweep, passing over the terrain of my life and searching for hidden and long-forgotten feelings. Oh, this happened when you were sixteen months old, and this happened when your dad beat the shit out of your brother or mother, or something more recent. Rebirthing is like cleaning out the basement after forty years and finding so many things that bring back the feelings of memories.

Overall, I found rebirthing a valuable tool for healing. After many sessions over more than ten years, I finally felt cleansed. By that, I mean that the pulling of the bow and releasing of the arrow no longer called forth uncomfortable emotions and memories. Instead, the breathing heightened awareness of a calm mind and a loving heart. It felt at that point similar to being given a clean bill of health.

Most people have absolutely no interest or desire to be rebirthed. Why would we want to bring up old shit when it runs contrary to our culture of avoidance? Yet, it makes perfect sense if we are interested in witnessing, feeling, and healing long-forgotten experiences. Rebirthing is a healing modality that has the potential to show us where, when, and how we developed unhealthy habits. Rebirthing can give us the opportunity to return to a particular section of the river that previously flipped us out of the boat. We have the opportunity to relive past experiences from a somewhat detached, higher perspective. This gives us the opportunity to go through, once again, the cold and turbulent waters of past difficult experiences without getting flipped out. It's a form of personal, internal cleansing. It is not easy, and it is always wise to have an experienced, trusting guide when venturing into previously unexplored territory.

As a result of my mother's depression, my father laid down strict rules. There were to be no heated discussions in the house—ever. Political and religious views were never mentioned for fear the emotional waves would disturb Mom. There was never a debate on any subject that I, as a child, could witness, let alone be a part of. School and the rules of the Church appeared to be much the same: "This is the way it is. Period!" There was no discussion of other beliefs, views, perceptions, or understandings. The "normal family emotional tide" was kept at such a minimum that my emotional body had rarely experienced turbulence. Even when Dad had a heart attack in 1964 and was hospitalized for two months, I don't remember feeling worried or scared. The brightest memory of Dad's stay in the hospital was watching the Beatles play for America for the first time on the Ed Sullivan Show while we were in my Dad's hospital room.

Out of some natural, protective choice, I developed the ability not to feel uncomfortable emotional waves, which doesn't mean they weren't present around me. It simply means that I learned to pay them no attention. No one ever talked about the unspoken, so how was I to know?

I didn't like homework or anything that had to do with spelling, reading, or taking tests, all of which were very uncomfortable for me. My parents never forced me to do homework or punished me for not doing it. I would make my body sick with a temperature of 99 degrees or above in order to miss school and be healed before the next baseball game or in time to play in the snow after the next big storm.

My brothers told me that I was getting away with murder compared to the strict thumb under which they had been raised. Things were different for me after the burn. If I was happy, Mom was happy. It was Mom who told the nuns in Catholic school that she would not take away my play time after school to do homework or punish me for getting bad grades.

Taking time to play and explore inner consciousness during the course of our daily lives is a discipline that leads to a greater sense of internal security in our later years. This I write as a sixty-five-year-old reflecting on certain stages of physical life and opportunity. What we seek, practice, and develop through our middle years eventually becomes the foundation of our consciousness in our older years. To pay it no attention, hoping that everything will be easier when we retire, is a misguided thought form of our consumerism culture.

Michael Carroll

Chapter 9:
SHAMANISM AND THE MEDICINE WHEEL

My protective emotional armor cracked.

A year past the Convergence, a friend in Santa Fe invited me to a men's weekend workshop given by a Medicine Woman. The essence of the teaching was man's imbalance with his female nature, and this was an introduction. I learned about my personal power animal and was introduced to the Shamanic practice of journeying into the underworld on the sound of a drumbeat. (The term shaman is interchangeable with medicine man/woman. They are the same, just as there is no difference between physician and doctor.)

We gathered in a circle. Once everyone was settled, the Shaman would light the sage or copal resin from a central fire; she'd smudge herself, the drum, and then the circle of people. The smoke was then passed around the circle and everyone smudged. Meanwhile, the Shaman began drumming to set the tone for the teachings. For those who have never experienced "smudging," it is an ancient practice in which the smoke from sage or copal resin is used to purify the energetic field around a person, place, or thing. If you have ever attended a Catholic High Mass, you will remember the priest walking down the center aisle of the church on his way to the altar while slowly swinging an incense holder on a chain back and forth, filling the church with its scent.

If only my school teachers could have captured my attention as the Shaman did that day! To say it simply: I loved the teachings. They ran alongside and then interwove with the experiences I'd had during my rebirthing sessions. We humans generally attribute the ability to feel and the sensitivity to emotion to females, yet, internally, it is the nagual part of us, our consciousness, where differences in our physical bodies don't matter because male and female are equal, and we are both. For me, coming to clarity about this was as big a piece of the picture as reincarnation and karma.

Journeying

After an hour or so of teaching, there was a pause for questions, and then we made the preparation to "journey." When we journey with the drum, we are entering the underworld. This underworld is not the dark place that you might associate with evil. It is the realm of the spirit animal, the place where our personal power animal can be our guide if we should choose to follow.

In a typical session, we would lie down, close our eyes, and as the drum beat out a steady rhythm, start looking for a cave, a hole, a body of water, or something like that. The idea was to find it, enter into it, and travel down through darkness until we eventually saw and entered the light of a new landscape. When we saw the landscape, we were to look for our power animal. Once we found our animal, we were to ask it a question we had formulated in our minds before starting the journey. Usually, it was a request for guidance in understanding something related to the teachings of the day. After a time, the drum rhythm would change, and that was the signal to wrap up the journey and return. When the drumming stopped, we would sit and be present in the circle.

One by one after my first experience, others told tales of their journeys, but I had nothing to say other than, "I didn't go anywhere." This went on for several years. I loved the teachings and eventually started participating in the sweat lodges when they came to northern New Mexico once or twice a year, but I always struggled with the journeying. My problem was that I was stuck in my head. Rebirthing had cracked this protective shell, and these native teachings were gently widening the cracks.

The Medicine Wheel

Woven in and through the fabric of these native teachings is the Medicine Wheel, the rolling wheel of our life. We are born into a certain direction or point on the wheel, and we spend the rest of our lives within the wheel. You can find out which direction you were born into (and your power animal) by studying the Medicine Wheel teachings or having a private session with a shaman, after which it will be clear.

Simply put, each direction holds a certain quality of energy that comprises the entirety of our being. As an example, the South is the place of children and the place of trust. The North is the place where we experience solitude and learn the inner wisdom of our True Self. The West is the place of dreams, introspection, and discernment. In the East, we find clarity and knowing that is beyond beliefs.

Maintaining the balance of our individual wheels is our personal responsibility. We might want to turn it over to Jesus or God, but the Earth teachings tell us that we are the keepers of our balance, and Mother Earth gives us ways to discover and experience it for ourselves.

• • •

Several years later, a workshop announcement that arrived by mail attracted my attention. It had something to do with the male and female warrior and the "little boy" and "little girl." Again, I absorbed the teachings. They made complete and perfect sense to me.

After having gone through the earlier workshops and rebirthing experiences, I was somewhat aware of my female presence and my little boy, but this little girl was new and something I had never considered.

In a group experience, we journeyed into the Medicine Wheel to look for our little boy, our little girl, our male warrior, and our female warrior. To the sound of the drum, I closed my eyes and drifted around in the darkness. An entrance to a cave appeared. I entered and moved into the darkness for a period of time, and then it happened—in full light and color, the landscape appeared and the dark cave vanished! I was in the mountains above my house in Pot Creek, walking toward a grass-and-wildflower meadow that I had visited often during my hikes. There in the center of the meadow was a Medicine Wheel.

As I approached the Wheel, a warrior appeared. No introduction was necessary. Together we looked at the Wheel from the East. We entered and turned North to meet the female warrior, who had just come into view. There was no doubt that she was the male warrior's equal and a part of me. When we looked to the West, our little boy appeared with a rush of great joy and happiness. Then, the little boy turned to face South, and the little girl appeared. Together, for a moment, we felt the wholeness. Then the drum changed its beat, and it was time to come back.

When I opened my eyes, the smile on the Shaman's face told me she knew I had journeyed. My previous difficulty traveling on the sound of the drum had vanished. It was a new revelation to experience journeying. It was quite different from the spiritual realm I had studied under the guidance of Herman. With Herman, we learned about the "Golden City" or "Shamballa" and the spiritual beings that lived and held "form" on higher, finer realms of existence. This watercolor by Herman of the spirit body leaving the physical connected by the golden thread is an example.

Although Herman talked of these experiences, his teaching focused on remaining present in the physical while trying to remember and feel the presence of the spirit in daily life. Our practice was always about transforming the ego personality into a channel for love and service. Techniques to leave our physical body were never taught or encouraged.

Now, with the sound of the drumbeat and conscious intent, I learned to enter the spirit-animal world, gather information, and return safely through the Shamanic practice of journeying. This made the camping trips I took to remote locations even more interesting!

In our early days of boat camping, Rick, Bernie, and I would set up our remote lake camp and then fish for twenty-four hours a day. We fished from the boat all day, and some evenings, too, with underwater fishing lights. Even when we were on land, our baited lines were in the water. Yes, we were a little obsessed. But really, this was just an indication of the little boy's and the warrior's need to be in Mother Nature.

Now that I had learned the native ways of journeying, however, I no longer wanted to fish after lunch. At first, Bernie and Rick made a fuss, but it didn't take long for those guys to agree. After fishing all morning, we would head back to camp, eat lunch, secure our lines in the water, put on daypacks, and go for a walk.

We looked for signs and gifts from Mother Nature while roaming the remote landscape. Over the years, we discovered special places to rest or to shelter out of the wind, rain, or sun.

During these periods, it was not unusual for us to make a simple altar on a flat stone, light sage, drum, unravel the cloth around the animal card deck, and give each other readings. Always we were learning about different animal natures, the directions they represented, and how they related to our present situation.

Vision Quest

By then, some number of years had passed, and in the fall of 1995, I was ready to go a little deeper into these teachings. I had been feeling stagnant, as if my inner river current was barely moving my raft, and I decided to reach out for some advice during a private session with the Shaman.

The analogy I used when presenting my dilemma to the Shaman was: "I feel stuck within the confines of a beautiful meadow. There is absolutely nothing wrong with this meadow, and yet I am simply looking for a way to quicken the pace of the current, or alternatively, get to the top of the surrounding mountain for a look around."

The Shaman suggested that I go on a four-day vision quest. Going on a vision quest had never crossed my mind. Had I ever known anyone who went on a quest? No. However, my instincts told me, as they did with the ideas of rebirthing and taking the second hit of mind-altering drug, that it sounded like a good idea, and I decided on the spot to do it. The instructions were simple: Go to a remote place in Mother Nature for four days and nights with no food or knife.

I prepared for six months by fasting frequently, cleaning up my diet, and doing a final intestinal cleanse that lasted fourteen days. I was doing all this while Michael Carroll Construction Company was taking off the roof of the old John Dunn House on Bent Street in Taos. Even before the project started, Polly, asked me to agree not to leave on a camping trip during the project. I did, and we as a crew managed to take the entire roof off the Old John Dunn House with shops underneath and add the dormers without a single drop of rain or one complaint! The pressure was off, and I was granted permission to go camping.

I am not quite sure how to start this story other than to say that, by chance, even with my busy schedule, the week I wanted to do the vision quest opened up. Before and after, work and life were hectic. I equipped myself with a blanket, sleeping bag, water, tarp, drum, tobacco, walking stick, and a hat.

Bernie offered to stay at base camp and drop off water once a day. We drove the truck and boat to the lake and then piloted the boat to the most remote end.

From there, it was a half-hour hike to the base of the high mesa rim. We hiked to the top of the ridge and headed northwest. As we walked, I asked my power animal to guide me to the spot. Eventually we arrived at a place with two boulders. They measured about four feet high, seven feet long, and six feet wide. I leaned my pack on a rock.

To the West was a juniper tree with a flat rock under it, the North was open, and the East had another juniper tree thirty feet away. The boulders completed the South side.

After I laid my pack down, I walked a bit further to see and feel if there was another better spot. There wasn't. When I came back, Bernie was thirty feet to the west, sitting on a rock that could be used as a tub if it rained enough. We lit sage, hugged, and then he walked away.

It was still morning and getting warm when the wind started to blow. I laid my blanket in the shade and took a rest. When I got up, it was still warm, so I took my clothes off except for my moccasins. I built a circle with rocks that would be big enough to contain a central fire, with enough space between the fire and the rocks for my sleeping bag and blanket. I started with the four directions and then filled in the rest until the circle felt complete. In the center, I made a fire circle. I gathered wood and set my blanket between the fire and the South.

At sunset, I lit the fire, and smudged myself, the drum circle, and a larger circle around the rocks and trees. I came back to the blanket and drummed for a short time. I asked for guidance. In a tired state, I lay down to gaze at the moon and stars in the clear sky. Sleep overtook me. During the night, I often woke up and placed a few more sticks on the fire. The wind was gentle and steady from the southwest. At some point, the wind stopped. When it returned, it was from the north; it had a colder bite and was accompanied by clouds.

At the first hint of dawn, I let the fire go out. The sun hitting my face brought me to a wakeful state; however, I was taken aback by how weak I felt when I first stood up. I found myself learning on a rock or lying down on another. It was hitting me that I had nothing to do: no coffee to make or food to eat, no one to call on the phone, and no place to go. I'd lean on a rock and drift off to no place or think about being there for three more days.

Seeking comfort, I took a walk to the ridge a few hundred yards to the south. I thought maybe I could climb down and get out of the wind, and it worked to some degree. When I started to feel small pains in the bottom of my stomach, I assumed they were hunger pains and tried not to think about it. Then, a loud voice that originated in my body started telling me a story I once read. In it, a grandma was sharing her knowledge about the body-mind and the spirit-mind with her grandson. My own body-mind was growing very loud.

The wind was getting colder. I could feel it starting to bite under my pullover, so I started walking while looking under juniper trees for incense. I'd crawl under a productive tree and pick pieces of the crystallized sap off the ground, one by one. When it was all collected, my situation came pouring back into my awareness. I headed back to my base.

When I got there, I put on my jacket and lay down on the blanket. The wind was getting stronger, and there was no comfort. I decided to try lying down in the stone tub, hoping it would stop the wind. It didn't. I got up and went back to the circle. I put the blanket down, got into my sleeping bag, and pulled it over my head. This warmed me up, and I lay there for hours.

There were still three hours to go before the sun went down, and I needed to drop off an empty water bottle so Bernie would know I was okay. I walked to our agreed spot. It felt good to see the three bottles he had left for me. I gave thanks to my friend.

When I got back, I again had to deal with the wind. I pulled some logs over and tried to make a wind block on the north side of the circle. It turned out to be useless—and worse, because the tarp created noise and got dirt on my face. By that point, I had accepted that I couldn't sleep in the inner circle. I thought maybe I could make a shelter between the two South rocks and the tree at the West. I longed for a tent and cursed out loud at the cold wind. To the north, the sky was looking black with impending cold rain or snow. I struggled to make this new shelter work because it was still inside the outer circle I had created. I thought it might work if I could just block the wind a little better. Close by and leaning on the west side of the South rock was a slab of rock that would do the job. I had moved it about six inches when it revealed a brown packrat about the size of a hamster and her three babies looking back at me. Everyone ran except one baby, who stared up at me and was the size of a regular mouse with big ears. I felt like an intruder and gently put the rock back.

By then, the sun was setting, and my vision quest had become a matter of survival.

I went to a boulder a few yards to the southeast. On its south side, the wind did not blow. I built a fire with a coal from the circle fire and managed to make a lean-to with my tarp. After placing my drum, blanket, and sleeping bag inside, I carried over wood for the fire and then crawled inside. The warmth and comfort the rock and fire gave me were pure pleasure, and I gave thanks. I alternately slept and kept the fire going.

The next morning, while the sun was still low in the sky, I crawled out of the shelter. I still felt weak, and I still had nothing to do except exist. I was grateful I had a walking stick to lean on. I went from rock to rock, resting, standing up, or lying down. The stomach pain had stopped, and hunger was not an issue. My challenge was how to keep my mind from wondering when this ordeal would be over. I couldn't stay upright for long; I was just too weak. Body aching, I lay back down in the shelter. I wanted to curl up and sleep, but sleep would not come. I had visions of starving people curled up, their big eyes looking back at me. I thought of the people I had seen with AIDS who had a hard time walking twenty feet. I started to experience a body-mind separation. I could find comfort outside of the body. There was a place to go. I was not just a body, which I always knew, but this experience had made it real.

When it was near noon, I felt strong enough to take a short walk. The wind was still cool. A battle of will was raging inside me. I kept thinking how nice it would be to have soup when I got back to camp. I was glad that I had told a few people that I was going for four days. It gave me the strength to keep going. "I can do this," I said to myself as I went back to the shelter. The sun seemed to stop in place. I'd doze off and think time had passed, yet, as I looked up at the sun through the tarp, it appeared that it hadn't moved. It became a waiting game. I wasn't worried about not having a vision. How could I when I was struggling so much?

At some time that afternoon, I decided to make friends with the wind. I asked the wind to please take away these thoughts of the past and future and bring me a vision. I was still in the shelter when the sun was just past mid-afternoon. I needed to drop off an empty water bottle so Bernie would know I was okay. I had the urge to roll some tobacco and smoke it. I did and took a few shallow puffs. I got up, put the water bottle and leather bag over my shoulders, and walked to our drop-off spot. He had left another bottle that I didn't need, but I took it, anyway. Looking down at my lakeshore base camp from the high mesa only caused pain. The fantasy of immediate relief was fruitless. I still had two nights to go.

When I made it back to the circle, I was still unsure if the weather would allow me to spend the night there. I gathered firewood and, just before sunset, I lit the fire and carried my blanket and sleeping bag to its place on the South side.

With the fire burning, I sat and drummed. For the first time, I sang; and for the first time, it came from a deep place within. I sang to the wind: "Oh, wind, carry my vision; take away the past and future." I was physically unable to stay in a good posture for very long, so I lay down and gazed at the moon and stars.

That night I dreamed. I was lying in bed with a woman, and as I became aroused, the dream changed. I was out of the bed and in a dark hall at the entrance to a large room. A woman appeared in front of me. She had the name of someone I once knew, but she didn't look like her. She was perhaps nine feet tall, and she had large breasts that were at my face level. I was not aroused.

Then, I heard song lyrics from the late Sixties: "Don't let the past remind us of what we are not now." I woke up and put a few more sticks on the fire.

When I awoke on the fourth morning, it was clear and warmer. Even though I was still weak, I did feel better. My head was full of the woman from my dream. I reached out to the wind. I said, "The past is like yesterday's weather and has no place with me on this quest." I asked the wind to help blow it away.

It was midday when I took a walk to the West. I hadn't gone far when I had a vision. In it, I was standing before a group of businessmen. It was a weekend workshop about the value of taking time off and remembering how to have fun. I thought that I couldn't do this, and as I did, it said, "If you can spend four days and nights in the wilderness with no food, you can stand in front of businessmen and teach them something about fun."

This vision was exciting because it came on its own and was the first thing of the kind that had happened to me in that realm. Another vision followed, indicating that I should buy a laptop and write. I continued my walk, feeling better than ever. I would lose myself under the junipers whenever I found one that had incense.

I came back to camp to rest. When the sun was low enough, I went to check on the water. It was there. I imagined myself at camp just beyond the hill. I could see the entrance to the cove. I allowed myself to dream for a moment as I burned some incense. The end was near. Vision or no vision, I had been given plenty, and I was grateful.

Back at the circle again, I began to pack and straighten up. It was my last night there, and I didn't want the shelter to remain after I was gone. When all was stowed, I knew that I would spend this last night on the north side of the circle. I was ready before the sun went down and started the fire. I used the larger logs, and as they burned, I pushed them in.

While sitting with a straight posture, I felt a surge of energy. I took off my shirt and moccasins and drummed. As I felt the energy rise, I called out from deep within and sang. When I stopped, I still felt good, and my back stayed straight. I was not tired. I added a few more sticks to the fire. I was sitting when a wave that seemed to come from the West hit me. I felt the urge to cry. I whimpered a few times as my consciousness went to my head. It seemed to remain close. I asked myself to go with it. The waves hit repeatedly, and each time I cried. Then, I began to cry out loud: "Open up my heart!" My hands peeled away at my chest as if to open my heart. I reached into the fire until my hands were hot and placed them on my chest. This I did many times.

I felt the urge to drum and journey to my animal. We met in a meadow and I got on his back. I wanted to open my heart. I pressed my chest to his neck, and it felt so good. I asked if he could show me a vision. We went in a circle in the meadow. Then, we were flying over the Taos Valley. We were circling the valley over the mountains to the east and then out over the gorge to the west. We went around many times, and when we stopped, we were in the southwest section of the Taos area.

I heard: "There is much in Taos to open up to—being confined to your meadow is no longer an issue." I saw a house with a sunroom and electric panels on the roof.

When the drumming stopped, I lay down for the night. The next morning, I awoke early, before the sun rose. After a trying four days and nights, I felt good and definitely in an altered state of consciousness.

I had a few hours left before leaving my camp. I got the fire going and finished packing up. Then, I took the Medicine Wheel apart and placed the rocks in spots where I felt they belonged. I still had a small stack of wood, and I knew when the last flame went out, Bernie would show up. It was so. My tasks for the morning were complete. I placed the last of the firewood on the fire and intently watched it burn until the last flicker of flame went out. I looked up and saw Bernie coming through the trees. We opened our arms to each other from a distance, and I felt him. We smudged the area and put the last of the sage on the coals, then watched it smoke until it burned out. I poured the last of my water on the fire.

I felt strong enough to carry my pack. We walked to the southeast corner of the ridge, and I followed Bernie down. I was once again glad I had a walking stick. When we were back at camp, I felt blissful. I laughed when I first tasted the potato, corn, catfish, and dumpling stew. I could hardly contain my excitement and joy!

Chapter 10:
DIVORCE CANYON AND THE MEDICINE SHIELD

A month after my Vision Quest, the John Dunn house remodel was complete and my family and the Bergersons rented a houseboat and camped at the end of a deep, remote canyon on Lake Powell. This trip also conveniently ended on the first day of my company fishing trip. As I was kissing my family goodbye at the marina after the family trip, I was also welcoming my crew and friends who were arriving for the company fishing tournament. Once all the boys had launched their boats, we drove about twenty-five miles south to a campsite at the end of Iceberg Canyon. They pitched their tents quickly, and before long, we were back in the boats and ready to go for a cruise. A few miles later, we stopped in the middle of the lake, tied our boats together, kicked back, ate some lunch, and took in the views. The three- to four-hundred-foot cliffs surrounding us were layered in tinted shades from grey to tan to salmon and contrasted sharply with the blue sky reflected in the waters from which they emerged. It was time for the guys to chill and unwind. They had started out before sunrise and driven four hundred miles to get to the lake.

We were minding our own business when the Ranger boat drove up to our boats and asked, "Is there a Michael Carroll here?" I was dumbfounded. What could he want with me? He told me straight out that my family had been involved in a single-car, rollover about fifty miles from the lake. Two children had been airlifted to the Grand Junction Colorado Hospital, and the others were at the Blanding Utah Health Clinic waiting for me. "How is my wife?" I asked.

"This is all the information I have."

There were no cell phones in those days, so we had to proceed with the anxiety of not knowing what was going on. We headed back to camp, and I packed up my clothes. Edwin dropped me off at the marina. I climbed in my truck and drove to Blanding, where I found Kathi, Michelle, and Amanda. Thankfully, they were all in one piece, having been treated for minor injuries and released. We drove to the junkyard to take a look at the car and then on to Grand Junction, the four of us in the front seat of my pickup. It was dark, and I remember there came a point when I was about to pass out from fatigue, and Kathi took over the wheel for the last hour.

The story was that Amanda's friend, Misha, had gotten a foot injury, and my daughter Jessica had been thrown out of the car during the roll-over. At first, Kathi had thought she was dead when she saw her lying still in the middle of the road. The helicopter arrived and the medics loaded up the two girls. Then, the helicopter wouldn't start! They were stranded on a two-lane road out in the middle of nowhere when a guy in a pickup truck drove up, got out, and asked, "Does anyone need help?"

The helicopter pilot said, "Our chopper won't start!"

The driver responded, "I am a certified helicopter repairman, and I got my tools in the truck." Unbelievable! The guy got the chopper started, and off it went.

When we finally reached the hospital and I got to look nine-year-old Jessica for the first time, she was asleep on the table, gauze bandages on her arms and legs and one on the top of her head. And yet, her face was untouched and beautiful. I was overcome with gratitude. She had sustained no internal damage, and her arm-and-leg road rash would be treated the same as third-degree burns. I was able to care for the wounds, but it didn't take long for Jessica to demand that she be the one to clean her wounds. Of course, I let her do so. She understood what needed to be done and did it herself, after which I helped her with the bandaging. There is more to the story, but I'll leave it by saying that I felt overwhelmed with gratitude. The impact of the roll-over had been minimal when I thought about what could have happened.

Life resumed, and I went through the rest of the summer and fall unaware that a major shift was about to occur in my life.

The Medicine Shield

By the following winter, I was jolted into another tight canyon with turbulent waters: my raft was heading for Divorce Canyon. It was a big deal and an extremely difficult section of the river for everyone. Boulders and rapids were everywhere, and visibility was low. It felt a little like taking the second hit of LSD and then asking Ray, "WTF is going on?"

This time, I reached out to the Medicine Woman for advice. She suggested that I build a Medicine Shield as a way to help me hold on to my power during the difficult times I was entering. I had never heard of a Medicine Shield and quickly learned that there are at least four kinds of shields, one for each direction on the Medicine Wheel.

This was the moment I became an apprentice. I trusted the Shaman's guidance without question. I felt like I had been thrown out of my boat into wildly rushing water that was over my head. I needed guidance on how to keep from drowning. I had no idea what I was getting into when I grabbed on to the idea of building a shield and was grateful for some instruction on how to keep myself from drowning. Someone was throwing me a lifeline. I grabbed on with relief and gratitude. I needed help.

In a simple and clear way, I was instructed on how to build a West Shield. I was told to dream the shield and then paint the dream on a skin. Immediately, I started to conger up how to make a dream shield with not much to go on, except that I should paint animals and symbols on a skin frame. First, though, I had to figure out exactly which animals to paint. Like being adrift in a fast and dangerous current, I was getting way too mental and feeling uncomfortable, to say the least. I needed stability and trusted enough to grab on to this idea of building a shield.

Healing Touch

That year marked my twenty-sixth year downstream from the familiar bridge of childhood, and beyond any doubt, I was traversing the most turbulent stretch of the river to date. The first few years during and after the divorce were extremely difficult. Externally, life went on. Luckily, my construction business and my relationships with all my subcontractors were running smoothly with competent employees. It also helped a lot that my clients, John and Pintki, were conscious souls who were perhaps fifteen years older than I. In another timely happenstance, Pintki was a well-experienced and wise energy healer. At the time, she was a teacher of the "healing touch" modality. So, I decided to let her work on me.

She was the first healer to soothe my energy without touching me physically. What do I mean by soothe? Imagine an intense time in your life when everything is moving really fast, both inside and out. It's like going down the rapids, one thing happening after another, and all that busyness takes over every waking hour of the day; or it's like pushing your raft into a river canyon that has no beaches or camping areas where you can pull over and rest for the night. In such a situation, you are lucky to find a boulder or a tree sticking out of the flooding waters that you can tie a rope to. And if you do, the water still flows forcefully under the boat, and there is no getting out. In the morning, just as soon as the your eyes open, the rope automatically unties itself and there you go again!

The energy healing I did with Pintki can be understood by visualizing a human body with energy radiating from it that extends out approximately three feet. This is called the energy field. Imagine that a body's healthy energy field is filled with millions of very fine, sensitive, energy hairs extending straight out, like a healthy, extra-long-haired, fluffy dog who has just been fully brushed. When we get stressed, our energy hair starts to lose its freshly combed, puffy feeling. Because of what I was going through, my energy hairs were all knotted up and matted when I walked into Pintki's healing room.

To begin, Pintki asked me to lie on the healing table in the middle of a beautiful room. We closed our eyes. She opened the energetic door by acknowledging the existence of healing presences in the room. Then she held her hand out about two or three feet over the body and felt the outer edges of my extended energy field, similar to how we hold our hands out toward a hot campfire to feel its heat. This is gentle. The healer does not want to enter into the energy field too abruptly. The healer feels the energy from a distance, as if just barely touching the surface, as you would if you were starting to detangle the coat of the dog. There is no reason to force the brush all the way to the skin and pull the comb down through the long hair on the first pass. It is the same with the energy field. In my case, it was going to take some time to untangle the knots.

The healer slowly raises her hands over the body, with the tips of the fingers hanging down into the energy field. Then, using her fingers like a rake or a wide-tooth comb, she slowly and gently stroked through my energy field from head to toe.

It didn't take long for me to start feeling my tension loosen. Pintki spent forty-five minutes combing me over and again before she was able to get to where the energy leaves the surface of the body. The worries, stress, and concerns of living through a divorce had knotted my energy, and, for the first time in close to a year, I experienced relief. Not just mild relief, but in the moment, it felt close to total relief, like finding a small island where I could stop, get out of the boat, and walk around; or like taking off wet cold clothes and feeling the joyful comfort of pulling on warm flannels. Mmm. This is what I meant when I said that the healer soothed me.

Yes, all the stuff I was dealing with was still there, but without the stress and tangles associated with it. Of course, my relief did not last forever. Just as the clothes we wear need to be washed, cleaned, and dried, so it is with our energetic body. I would need more sessions as I went through the divorce, but I was pleasantly surprised by the energetic impact of the healing on my state of consciousness. Over the next few years, I took classes in healing with Pintki.

During this difficult period, my clients, including Pintki, told me directly that they understood what I was going through, and at the same time, Pintki referred to me as a "master builder." She was the only person ever to say that I was a master, but I suppose on some level I was. I was near the peak of a good building career in Taos, and my crew and subcontractors at the time knew what they were doing and got along very well with both the owners and the designer. Had my clients been difficult, that would have complicated my situation even more. The owner and designer both knew and accepted that I wasn't getting out of Divorce Canyon any time soon. Again, I felt immense gratitude.

Dreaming My Shield

I always needed ways to soothe and rejuvenate the essence of my life, and I was deeply grateful to own a boat and have the ability to camp in remote areas, because it always achieved that end. In those days, I enjoyed walking in the wild lands surrounding the lakes, keeping on the lookout for all the different animals that crossed my path, from rattlesnakes to eagles and everything in-between. By then, I was six months into dreaming my shield. Its physical shape was starting to take form as I drew my ideas in a sketchbook. I placed different animals at the different directions to see how it felt while I waited for a sign from Spirit to help me move forward.

One time while we were remote camping, my buddy, Mark, decided to spend a day and night alone. In the morning after he left, I decided to go fishing. I was on the front of my boat, using the electric trolling motor, when I pulled into the back of Turtle Cove. I looked into the water and saw a turtle shell a few feet below the surface of the water. I was excited. A turtle shell—what a gift! I got down on my knees, and as I reached into the water, I saw that a stick had been jammed through its shell. It was a letdown. I thought the damaged shell might not be a good medicine piece. I grabbed it, took the stick out, and went back to camp on the other side of the lake. Soon, I felt the urge to take a hike with my drum.

I was in no rush and had no particular place to go. I walked until a feeling indicated that this was the spot. I smudged myself and the drum and then closed my eyes, sinking into the deep sound of the drumbeat. Right away, I entered into the journey time. I was ten years old, back in West Paterson, at our family-gang summer picnic. While I had been playing in the brook, I found a turtle about the size of my hand and carried it back to the picnic area to show it to a girl who was about my age. The turtle was crawling on the ground when I picked up a pipe and pushed it through the turtle's shell. The girl yelled, and I laughed it off. I did feel bad after killing the turtle, but I didn't show it.

The Spirit of the turtle started talking to me as I sat and drummed. He told me that he had been grateful for the opportunity to take the pipe through his back then, and so today, I could have the experience of communicating with him. This was the clear sign I had been seeking. Turtle would be the first animal on my shield. I would paint it at the South, where turtle is from. At last, I had a starting point.

On another occasion soon after, while I was remote camping and fishing on Navajo Lake, I hooked onto an eight-pound northern pike. Normally, I let caught fish go, but this one swallowed the hook and died in the fish livewell. It was then that I got the urge to hike to the top of the cliffs and offer the fish to the big birds.

I tied the boat off and started hiking, the thirty-three-inch fish hanging off the end of my walking stick. After some effort, I reached the top and placed the fish on the furthest edge of the rock cliff overhanging the lake. Then I found a comfortable spot in the shade and started drumming. It was not long before an eagle bigger than me appeared. Standing before me, it opened its wings and embraced my body within its folds. A moment later, when its wings went back to its side, the eagle's left eye popped out of its socket and was offered to me so I could see from above the mountain. Like the turtle, this was a powerful message. I prayed to the eagle and asked for its medicine to bring clarity of sight to both the bigger picture and the fine details of my life.

Finally, I felt I was getting somewhere with the shield. Years earlier, when my river was running smooth, I had established a relationship with the horse and the elk. The elk had come to me on a below-zero

Friday night around eleven p.m., when my daughter, Amanda, had returned home from a date. She told me there was an injured elk on the side of the road a few miles back. She and her date showed me. It was a huge, bull elk with a large rack. It had two broken legs and a loose rack on its skull that moved from side to side as the elk squirmed and struggled to stand up on its mangled legs. I owned an over-under, single-shot 22/20-gage rifle, so I went back home to pick it up.

It took two slugs to kill the elk. I had never shot an animal before, aiming at its chest. A few seconds after the slug entered, a huge plume of hot steam shot twenty feet into the night from the nickel-size hole where I had shot him in the lung. I reloaded and shot him in the neck. It was over. It was over for the elk, but I still had to deal with the results of two phone calls I had made at the house when I was getting my rifle. I had called my construction foreman, Art, because he was a hunter and would know what to do with the elk, but I'd had to leave a message. I had also called the state police because I didn't want the elk to be left to the coyotes and birds.

In the meantime, Art showed up and started gutting the elk. Next, the state trooper showed up and said the game warden was on his way. The cop told me it was illegal to kill the elk but that he would have done the same thing. It was not an issue. The temperature dove below zero at midnight, and just as Art finished all the work, the game warden came and we loaded the elk in the pickup. I asked if I could have the ivory tooth in the bull elk's mouth. The others thought nothing of it and pulled the tooth for me. It was one of my first medicine pieces. And so, the elk was my fourth animal.

With these four animals—turtle, eagle, elk, and horse (whose back I had ridden on in my Vision Quest), the major four directions were covered. The turtle would be in the South and the eagle in the North. The horse would be in the West and the elk was of the East. It had taken six months to get the four directions lined up, and it would be another year before I completed the Medicine Shield.

I still needed to fill in the other spaces on the shield. I began in the Southeast, by painting a teepee with eight doors. In my own way, I was honoring my building career, which had generated enough cash that I could raise my children in a relatively comfortable way.

In the Northeast, I painted a circle, within which I saw myself leading a small council in these native ways.

The Northwest showed me sitting with my inner council of chiefs, who would assist me in journey time. From them, I could seek advice and receive different perspectives on a particular situation.

In the center, I painted the tree of life. Above the tree roots and below the branches, I painted my inner male and female warriors, the sword of truth hanging above their heads.

I was so close to completing the shield. The Shaman was pushing me along by then. Enough was enough. It was time. She said to finish the shield and get it into the ground.

Rooting My Personal Power

As I said in the beginning, the basic intent behind the Shield was to root my personal power in Spirit and help me in meeting my True Self. I was told that I needed to keep my ego out of the shield, because whatever was painted on the shield would magnify ten thousand times. I understood. My shield process was extending into overtime, and she had given me a little guidance to move me along. I added the eight skulls as awareness of our physical mortality and the water snake to symbolize the river of life and to act as a container for the dream.

It was around the time of the longest day of the year, and I was 99 percent ready to bury the shield. As I remember, I hooked the boat up to the truck and drove to the lake early in the morning. I went to the same beach on which I'd camped on the day I returned from the Vision Quest. There, in the boat, I painted the final symbols within the Southwest circle. I wrapped the shield in cotton fabric and hiked to the remote place of my Vision Quest. There, I dug a hole in the Earth about three feet deep and buried the shield in a simple ceremony.

I walked back to the boat, went back across the lake, and drove back to Taos. I had been told that I would become "pregnant" with the shield, and that I should dig it up when I felt ready to give it birth. I had buried it in June, and now it was a few days before Christmas. I felt it was time.

I was the only one to leave tracks in the snow covering the boat-ramp parking lot. It was cold, maybe thirty degrees. The boat's motor started. The lake was calm and glassy and giving off a steaming mist because the water was warmer than the air. I traveled to the remote end of the lake, tied off the boat, and hiked with my shovel for about forty-five minutes. I dug up the shield and took it home.

At that time, I lived on the Taos Mesa off of Millicent Rodgers Road. A few friends were aware that I was working on something in the teepee I had set up in the backyard, but I never spoke of the details. The shield work, during its creation and manifestation, is private work, and I had been instructed not to share it with others. No one would have understood, anyway. I had my good teacher who lived in a third-world country to guide me. I wrote her a letter every few months and got a response several weeks later. Mostly, I talked with inner guides and developed more consciousness of my nighttime dreams. Everything was in play. No longer could I separate my life into the different compartments of work, relationships, personal time, and recreation.

I had wrapped the shield in several layers of cotton cloth and it had been buried for six months, so there was some damage to the Southwest section of the shield that I repaired with elk-skin thread and painted. I hung my Medicine Shield in my teepee, but I kept it covered when others were present.

Chapter 11:
THE UNBURIED SHIELD

I didn't know what I had created. For sure, it wasn't a magic cure, since my difficulties continued. In fact, they were intensifying! It seemed that I had no roots touching the Earth. Again, I reached out for guidance, and when the response returned, I was told that the shield I had created was energetically above my head when it should be energetically under my feet! Again, I was grateful for the insight, but how was I supposed to get this thing to be under my feet? It wasn't like I could take it off the wall and step on it. I no longer had any doubt that this shield of mine had a life of its own and that I had to deal with it, take responsibility for it. The first thing on my list was to start disciplining myself with a deep, rooting, breathing exercise. Every day for half an hour, I sat and breathed up through my root to my second and third energy centers and then reversed it.

As I breathed in, I found it helpful to visualize my root center as window screen. I imagined seeing and feeling the flow of energy coming up from the Earth, passing through the screen and into the red-colored root chakra, and then continuing up through the orange second chakra just below the navel, and then into the yellow third chakra in the solar plexus. Then I paused and reversed the flow of energy back into the Earth, paused again, and repeated the process.

I had been told to keep the breath within these lower three chakras, with no breath above the third chakra during this time. That guidance was impeccable, because I was in desperate need of grounding roots. Had I been instructed to breathe up through my crown chakra, I believe the results might have been disastrous.

I flashed back to my days in Gainesville. Then, and still to this day, I've observed that well-intended personalities get spaced out or disconnected mentally and emotionally after learning and practicing advanced energy and breathing exercises prematurely. There is no rush. A true guru or shaman has the ability to read an individual's energy field. He or she knows where you are mentally and emotionally, just as a high-quality physical trainer knows which exercise to prescribe next in a cohesive, custom training program.

The effects of breathing into the lower three chakras were starting to take hold like seeds sprouting in good soil. Gradually, I was coming back into my body, and gradually, the shield that had been above my head found its place on the ground and under my feet. That was when I felt a strong urge to journey to the turtle and ask for guidance. As usual, I smudged, reached out to the Great Spirit, and started drumming. The turtle appeared and immediately explained that I needed to actually enter the energy of the shield and learn to move with it. To do this, I had to travel around the shield's eight directions to fully enter and live in the center of the shield. Then, I was invited to climb on the shell and go for a walk. The turtle understood that I had no idea what I had created energetically and explained a little about how to deal with it.

I was told to enter the shield from the South on the back of the turtle and learn to feel the energy of internal stability and its connection to Mother Earth. I had to trust that this would work out even though I had no idea where I was going or what I'd be getting myself into.

Shamanic Retreat in Chiapas, Mexico

During this period of working with my Medicine Shield, I was invited to Chiapas, Mexico, for a twenty-one-day total disconnection from my American life. As in all the other such trips I had taken, my perspective of the world would clearly expand and would remain expanded forever. In these remote, third-world areas, the people are very close to the Earth. They do not live in public housing; instead, they live in shacks they've managed to build by scraping together the materials. This Chiapas village was the poorest of the poor worlds I visited. They lived mostly on corn-water soup. Other communities were more alive and colorful.

While there, I fasted with the warriors and helped them prepare the lodge for the sweat. For hours, they kept the rock-filled fire going until all the rocks for the sweat glowed red when they were placed in the center of the lodge. The first round was hot, and the second round was equal to the hottest sweat I've ever experienced in the States. Then, it got hotter still as more fiery-red rocks were added during each round. I was astounded by how they could remain sitting straight-backed with head held high in such heat. By the third round, my nose was on the ground as I sniffed for the coolest air, which was closest to the dirt. Later, I was told that enduring the sweat is like lying on a bed of nails: you have to put it out of your mind. As in martial arts, there are many levels. It takes years before certain new awarenesses are revealed to the disciple, student, or apprentice.

Learning Native Council Ways

When I returned to my daily life in Taos, I had a new focus, and soon managed to purchase a piece of land bordering the national forest. I built a house, built a pond, and leveled out by hand an area for a Medicine Wheel and an eighteen-foot teepee. In my spare time, I collected willows by the river to build a sweat lodge.

In other words, I had a lot of energy. I did this while I ran the construction company and played hardball in the men's adult league. For housing, I lived and slept in a twelve-foot teepee at the edge of my land next to the national forest.

During that time, I agreed to take on the responsibility of hosting the Shaman's workshops in the fall of 1999. This marked the beginning of my learning native council ways and how they govern as a people. This was the birthing time of the Taos Council, which included three women in the northern New Mexico area who had also been following the teachings of the Shaman for some years. Together, we formed a circle, each member representing one of the four directions. Our first order of business was preparing the way for the upcoming workshops, sweats, and private sessions visitors would have with the Shaman.

It was a busy and enjoyable summer, living in the teepee. In early fall, my adobe house had windows, doors, and a roof. The finish work had yet to begin, but I did manage to get water to the toilet and a sink in a makeshift cabinet. The kitchen had a plug for the refrigerator, a gas outlet for the stove, a rough kitchen counter, and a sink. The workshops and sweats came and went with good success, and a new and stronger commitment had been forged among the council members to continue gathering and practicing these medicine ways for another year.

At that time, I was the only council member to have visited Chiapas and participate in the council ways in the Mayan Zapatista land. And I had plans to visit once again in the late winter or early spring of 2000.

This was all happening very fast, and yet, although the current of my life was swift, it was also wide, with no narrow or twisting canyons in sight. I was now abiding in the Southeast of the shield, where I had painted the teepee with eight doors. Indeed, I felt at home for the first time in a very long time.

Apprentice Training in Mexico

In the winter of 2000, I settled into a new rhythm. The current slowed, and my way was wide and clear. I felt the roots of the turtle energy taking hold. I was stronger when I visited Chiapas in the spring for my second year in a row.

This trip started differently, right from the start. I wasn't picked up at the airport in Tuxsula by the Shaman and her partner, as I had been on my first trip. Instead, a Mexican driver holding a sign with my name on it was there, waiting. I didn't speak Spanish, and he didn't speak English. I trusted him, and I arrived at the Shaman's house a few hours later.

The main purpose of this particular trip was to be trained as an apprentice and to experience a deeper level of involvement with the local people. In addition, I would be learning more about dealing with council business back in Taos.

The Hole

Toward the end of my first week, I was introduced to "the Hole." Until then, I had never heard of it. Sometime between this session and the one last year, the Shaman's partner and friend had built a small hut that was ten feet in diameter and about thirty inches up off the ground to keep the rain out. In the middle of the hut was a small, round rug. When the rug was lifted or pulled to the side, it exposed a wooden manhole-type cover. To remove the cover or slide it to the side required getting down on your hands and knees. Removal of the wooden cover revealed a black hole with a ladder descending seven feet down into a five-foot diameter, round hole of pure Mother Earth.

The next morning, I entered the hole with a blanket, a water bottle, and a drum. Once I was settled, the Shaman slid the wooded cover over the hole and then moved back the rug to keep the light out. I had agreed to stay for twenty-four hours. Talk about trippy! The only entertainment available was journeying into the underworld with my drum or repositioning my 70.5-inch body comfortably in a 60-inch diameter circle. Once I settled in with my blanket and found a comfortable position, I noticed three things almost at once: the first was that it was so dark that it didn't matter whether my eyes were open or closed; the second was the dead silence except for the sound of my breath and heartbeat; and last was how loud my thinking mind was getting.

In effect, I was blind and deaf. What do you do when there is nothing to do, see, or hear? As for me, I thought about everything: work, relationships, family, kids, past experiences, and my situation down there in the Hole in Chiapas. I soon discovered that there was a limit to how many times I could think about one particular situation in my life before it eventually burned itself out. But when it did, I would be on to another internal conversation. This was similar to the experience on the Vision Quest when I was reminded of the grandmother telling the story about the body mind and the spirit mind.

And once again, my body mind was quite loud. At least on the Vision Quest I could look for incense under the trees, collect firewood, walk to the water drop-off spot, look at the sky, build a fire, or feel the change in climate. The Hole takes the volume level of "no distractions" down to a new low. It was a good eighteen hours before the major chitchat inside my head started to calm down. And that was when things started to get a little trippy. With no light and no sound and no thoughts—what is left? Out in the distance, I heard someone call my name. The twenty-four hours had ended.

Later that afternoon, there was a sweat, and the next day we were off to another village. On other days, we had council meetings when we (mostly they) gathered and discussed the community projects we were involved with. The meeting was in Spanish, and the Shaman translated. When there were decisions to be made, the questions would be clarified, and then everyone would journey on the sound of the drum. When we returned, as in a workshop, we sat in a circle and listened to what each person had to say. In other words, we integrated the advice of Spirit into the business of our daily lives.

I was experiencing and actually participating in "council ways." I learned that members of the council sit in the various directions of the circle, each in the direction that most closely aligns with their true nature. As an example, if a member of the council had a hummingbird for a power animal, you would not find this person sitting in the North. She would be naturally comfortable in the South or East, while a wolf would be more at home in the North, and a bear would be at home in the West.

This I witnessed as a most beautiful approach to problem solving for the greater good of all concerned. Other animal spirits were represented, such as the rattlesnake, the eagle, the coyote, the raven, the elk, the hawk, the buffalo, the beaver, the vulture, the owl, the deer, and the horse. There were more, of course, but these were the main players in the story.

Forty-Eight Hours in the Hole

Near the end of my three-week trip, I was offered the opportunity to have another Hole experience. This time, I suggested that I stay in the Hole for forty-eight hours. It seemed to me that twenty-four hours was not quite long enough to get the full experience. In my first experience of the Hole, it had taken at least eighteen or more hours for my wild thinking mind to run out of gas. After adding the hours of sleep, twenty-four hours ended entirely too soon. And so, I climbed down the hole, prepared to stay there for forty-eight hours.

• • •

Once again, I thought about everything imaginable for hours and hours until eventually the thoughts burned out. The difference this time was that, instead of having only six to eight hours left in the Hole after my mind quieted, I still had thirty-two hours left to be alone with my Self without the overwhelming distraction of thoughts.

What takes over once the thoughts stop? Who are we once the thoughts stop?

It was a little weird when I couldn't tell if I was dreaming or awake. I couldn't see the dirt wall or my hand in front of my face, but I certainly could see the scenes as they played out in my mind's eye like a vivid dream or movie. It was profound for me as a person. It didn't matter if my eyes were open or shut.

When I heard my name, Michael, it was time to climb up the ladder and return to the surface of the Earth. I was informed that this would be another good day to sweat with the Chiapas warriors.

As before, the fire burned for many hours until the rocks were red-hot. I was not the same person who a year earlier had needed to put his face on the Earth in search of cooler air. This time, I was able to hold my posture and stay focused with the warriors for the full four rounds. When the sweat was over, we shared a delicious feast. That was when I noticed a shift among the warriors. I could tell that they appreciated my ability as a guest to go deep with them. It felt good for me as well to connect with these men and hold my own. I was blessed by the Shaman to lead sweats in Taos.

Deborah and the Garden of Eden

When I returned to Taos, I felt exceptionally good on all levels.

One of the first things I did was to call Deborah. We had dated just once, on the night before I left for Chiapas. I do admit that I had thought about her often when I was in the Hole. We were connected on many levels, and we took "fun together" to a new level, one that neither of us had ever experienced in a relationship.

We camped at Concha Lake during the first week of May and experienced what we felt to be the Garden of Eden. We were also together on what we called the "cosmic" night, the evening that the Taos sunset was in perfect alignment with the smoke coming from the Los Alamos fire. The colors that evening were so out of the ordinary that we pondered for a moment whether this might be our last night on Earth. Who really knew what dangerous nuclear material could be burning?

We survived, as did everyone else, and continued to enjoy a most wonderful summer together. We saw Steely Dan in concert when they opened the New Journal Pavilion in Albuquerque that summer, and later that summer, we saw Sting in the same venue and agreed it was one of the best concerts of our lives. In fact, the year 2000 was one of the greatest years of my life. However, by late summer, the preparations for my second year of workshops and sweat lodges required attention.

The workshops came and went, and in the aftermath, they left a new and deeper commitment to the practice for all of us council members. After the workshops, some who had participated requested to take part in the Taos council teachings and sweats in the upcoming year. Thus, the council expanded to include not only the inner core council, the original four who had been gathering bi-weekly, but also a new group of outer core members who would attend the monthly teachings and sweats that were taking place every three months at the beginning of the spring, summer, fall, and winter seasons.

Commitment

As we entered the early winter of 2001, the council was developing strong roots at the same time I was moving from the Southeast teepee in the Medicine Shield to the East, the place of the elk. Big difference! Not only was it a change in direction, but it also had the added big energy of the elk. Think of the South and its essence of trust; add the turtle with its slow, easygoing introduction to the entrance of the shield; and then compare that to what is called the "light of the mind" in the East joined with the strength and stamina of the elk to go the distance, and you are in a completely different situation.

What had been a smooth, easy, and pleasurable transition from the South to the Southeast was not to be like my experience heading into the East. All the fun with Deborah had ended as the river we had enjoyed together diverged. I felt clear about my commitment to the council and the native path I was walking. The Taos council was in full swing, with active inner and outer councils. It was during this period that I was contacted by the council leader on the East Coast who held the same position I did. She was a sister who asked me if I would take her to a remote place for her vision quest in New Mexico.

This was also a time when I was forced to hold my ground with a client while I was building his million-dollar house. He accused me of taking too much time off from his job. There was no problem on the job site; he simply didn't like the fact that I took time to go camping. As I remember it, I had visited the job site in the morning to be sure everyone was lined out for the week before I headed south to pick Susan up at the airport. That's when the cell phone rang. It was the owner. He yelled at me and then told me that he didn't like me taking time off from his job. Politely, I told him that I was presently off on another trip and that I would be back on the job on Monday. Then I asked, "Was there a problem on the job?"

"No," he answered. "Only that you take too much time off."

We got to the remote part of the lake, and the next day, Susan took off on a four-day quest. This left me alone at base camp for four days. Although I had coffee, food, and a tent, I was alone and forced to deal with my client, who had erupted inside my head. The conversation got very loud. It was a battle similar to the one I had on my Vision Quest. By the morning of the fourth day, the intense conversation still plagued me until I almost stuck my hand into a rattlesnake while gathering firewood. I was just reaching down and moving closer when the snake came into focus. I jumped back.

The hypnotic hold of the thoughts and inner conversation with my client was broken, and they began to dissolve, similar to the way my thoughts had burned out when I was down in the Hole. By the next morning, I felt strong and clear, and my inner conflict with my client was over. I walked to the top of the ridge to greet Susan, who was returning to the world the morning after her Quest.

When I returned to the jobsite on Monday, not a word was spoken by the owner about the conversation we'd had on the way out of town a week earlier. Everything on the job site was as smooth as it was when I had left. In fact, it was even better, because the tension between the owner and me was gone.

The summer faded as the 2001 seminars overlapped with the 911 World Trade Center collapse. Plans to fly east to assist the Shaman for another round of teachings were cancelled. As we all remember, it was an intense time. For the council, it was a sign to dive deeper into commitment.

By the time the workshops were over and air travel had resumed, I had arrived in the Northeast circle of my shield, where I had painted the medicine council. I spent the remainder of that year and most of the next learning council ways and practicing together as a group.

By late fall of 2002, the Shaman's teachings and sweat lodges had once again passed through my backyard. In the aftermath, my inner waters had shifted. It was clear that I was walking a lonelier path. During this period, an elder sister left the inner council for reasons I respected, and a much younger apprentice took her place.

By late December, I was somewhere high up on a northern mountain trail when I had a dream. The Shaman's partner, who was a Mayan Indian, appeared in my dream with a tobacco pouch. We sat together, rolled a smoke, and passed it back and forth. When we finished, we both got up and walked away in opposite directions, alone. There was no Shaman, and there were no female apprentices. This was such an unusual dream that I mentioned it to the Shaman. Shortly, I received a letter. Things were changing. The Shaman had separated from her partner and was with another man who had deeper connections into the Zapatista world.

I think she was a bit surprised that I had been able to receive such a dream and suggested that she visit my home in Taos toward the middle or end of February of 2003 for several weeks, after which I would return with her to Chiapas for several more weeks. I was 100 percent engaged in the flow of this Medicine Path, the council, and its conscious efforts to help raise a small amount of cash for improving the lives of the Mayan people.

A Silent War in the Mayan Lands

When the Shaman arrived, she was in need of rest, so no workshops were open to the public. It was a wonderful opportunity for the Taos council. We talked much about the movement in Chiapas to improve the Mayan people's way of life and the active role of the Chiapas Council.

When I returned to Mexico with the Shaman, the situation was quite a bit different from my previous two trips. I was taken deep into the third world once again, however, this time I was also learning about the silent war. The fun and games were over. I was now the male warrior from the States. It was easy to note that, in Taos, I was the only male in a women's council, while in Chiapas, the Shaman was the only female in a council of men.

I was in Chiapas when our country invaded Iraq. As I remember it, the newspaper headline read: "America against the World." The papers were also not afraid to publish photos of what we call in the States "collateral damage." I could only imagine how different things would be if we in the States were allowed to see the reality or the damage caused by our weapons.

In the Mayan lands, where most everyone looked the same in their manner and dress, Other than a very minor military presence, a silent, undercover war was taking place in which there was no way to know from outer appearances who was on whose side. I had come to learn that villages had separate alliances with the different leaders in power.

One day, we visited a church in a remote village square. You are not to take pictures in the church. The Shaman had my camera and did not realize that the flash would go off automatically in the dark church. Within moments, elders of the church and people from the village had surrounded us. The Shaman gave me the camera and said, "Don't give it to them."

We were surrounded for about fifteen minutes. I had zero understanding of what was being said. Then, four or five of the elders led us around to the back of the church. We settled the camera-flash incident for a few hundred pesos, or about thirty bucks. The Shaman told me to give them the money, and we were let free.

Once back in the car, I learned that we were in deep shit until our guide, the Shaman's boyfriend, and the village leaders came to the understanding that we were all on the same side. There was no doubt in my mind now that the mother council was involved in a cause. I should also say that never once did I witness any act of aggression.

The next day we were in a very poor, remote village, where I was served corn water soup as a guest. Later in the day, the men took me into an area where there were a few trees. One man filled his mouth with water and then blew it into one of the quarter-inch wormholes in a tree. In a few moments, a large, fuzzy worm came out. They fried it on the rocks by the fire and gave it to me to eat. And it was good, sort of. They considered it dessert and were honored that I ate it.

There was a community that grew coffee beans. I learned that it takes ten months for coffee beans to mature and that, until the Shaman's council became involved, the poor, remote community had had no way to deliver the beans to market. They had to rely on a truck owner from outside to pick up and deliver the beans to market. Unfortunately, the owner of the truck was not an honest man, and after ten months of the villagers' hard work, he took 50 percent of the profits for himself. With the assistance of the council, the community obtained a used pickup truck and was able to reap the full 100 percent profit from their labor. The truck also enabled the village leaders to travel to the city for supplies. This was just one more eye-opener into the reality of third-world existence.

The best I could tell, the silent war had to do with abuse of natural resources and the great imbalance due to the overpopulation of an undereducated group of people who lived well below what we in America consider poverty.

Journeying in the Hole

In between our adventures into the third world, time was set aside for rejuvenation, which included visiting the remote-site sweat lodges and holes.

On this trip, I had the pleasure of going down into the Hole on two occasions, each for forty-eight hours. By then, I knew the process: I'd go down into the darkness and listen to all the thoughts running through my mind until they eventually burned out and my mind was clear and calm. This was like the moment in a theater when the lights go out and the movie starts playing on the big screen.

On the sound of the drum, I found myself under the tree of life and almost instantly began to sink down into the roots of the tree. There, under the roots, I saw the turtle. He opened his mouth, and I thought, "He wants to eat me," so I backed away. Then, I had the urge to travel to the council of chiefs in the shield's Northwest sector for advice, but I discovered I could not reach the chiefs from the Hole. So, I went back and faced the turtle to see what he might do or say. The turtle came close, and once again opened his mouth. This time, I walked into his mouth and then down into his belly. That was when I understood that I could enter the turtle's belly—not to be eaten, but for my own protection.

In time, I walked out of his mouth, and then I saw and connected with a different turtle. It was the turtle in the South on the shield, the same one whose shell I had ridden upon in a vision five years earlier. Right away, the turtle reminded me of trust and death. Then, the scene changed, and we were in Turtle Cove. We were on land, but obviously this land had been under water when the lake was higher a year or two earlier. I saw a dried-up turtle shell. Flash! I flashed back to the second turtle shell I found during a camping trip sometime shortly after I buried the shield. This turtle shell was located on dry land, where a lake had once been. What made this shell so special was the way it was discovered, with the dried bones of the body laying alongside and within the shell itself.

I was in journey time, and the turtle shell with bones was as big as the living turtle whose mouth I had just walked out of. I had felt no hesitation when entering the shell, and I understood without words that I could come here in journey time when there was need to call upon Mother Earth for protection.

At the next drumming, the intent was to journey to the West to find the horse with the rainbow blanket. A brown horse with a rainbow blanket was walking toward the center of the shield, and because the horse's walk was much faster than mine, I had to run to catch up so I could jump on. In the center of the shield, I met the female warrior I had painted. We embraced and merged; it was as simple as that. Then, the scene changed. Looking up, I saw that the sword of truth was hanging over my head. For the first time, I understood what had been causing my problems. I was trying to see the woman in the shield as my external mate, when in fact, she had been my internal mate all along. I grabbed the sword.

I was on the horse as he galloped down a road into increasing darkness. We then descended until we were in the roots of the tree at the center of the shield. This time, I was holding the sword. A vision came in the form of a superbly crafted arrow that had bones hanging from it. It was said that the arrow with the hanging bones represented all of the weapons that I carry within, whatever they might be.

Again, I drummed, intent on visiting the horse in the West. This time, as a traveler focused on his destination, I was ambushed by a woman with whom I'd had a run-in during the creation of the shield. Her name was Crazy Woman, and she had a powerful influence on my perception of the sacred feminine. I had been walking alone when she captured me, tied me on the ground, and proceeded to build a fire on my chest. Once I surrendered to my fate, I was told that she was doing this to open my heart.

At once, I was riding my horse toward the center of the shield, my heart ablaze with love. In the middle of the shield, under the tree, the two of us merged again and were no longer separate. As one with the sword, we went down into the roots, and from there, we dropped further downwards and found a cave. The large woman I had met during my Vision Quest, whose breast was at my face level during the quest, appeared. She told me to remember the song from my vision quest: "Don't let the past remind us of what we are not now." I took that to mean that, once again, I am as changed as I was after the Vision Quest, and that the past is just a goodbye. It felt good, and with a heart full of love, I walked forth.

When the forty-eight hours had passed, it was time to come back to the surface and prepare for a sweat. On this occasion, I was asked to lead the first three rounds of the sweat with the Chiapas warriors. When I left Chiapas, I felt strong.

A Clash of Purposes

Soon after, another council member from Taos went to visit Chiapas for her first experience and returned with the new message: "The Taos Council's purpose is to help the Mayan People."

Let me say here that in all the workshops, teachings and experiences I'd had up until this very moment with the Shaman, I had felt no conflict with what was being said or passed along—until then. The words: "The Council's purpose" flipped a switch that reminded me of my connection with Herman's teachings, in which I had understood that my purpose was to become a clear channel for the light and love of Christ."

Hearing the word purpose in relation to the council brought everything into focus in a new light, similar to seeing the rattlesnake just as I was about to grab a piece of wood during Susan's Vision Quest.

When I heard the statement: "The Taos Council's purpose is to help the Mayan People," I voiced to the council: "That is not my purpose." I spoke to this directly because I had always felt that my purpose with the council was aligned with the possibility of helping my brothers and sisters in the States understand the wisdom of these native ways. I had never once thought otherwise.

Also, as a recreation major in college and the lover of many different games over the years, I've always had a natural reaction and objection when someone tries to change the rules in a game I am involved in without a discussion and my consent. When that kind of thing happens, I believe anyone involved can freely choose to say: "The game is over. I am not playing anymore, unless of course we all agree to the rule change."

The statement by the Chiapas Council was a bit of a surprise, but one I easily understood. The Shaman's life had changed from the time we had met some fifteen years earlier. Now, she was involved in the Mayan cause at the grassroots, by helping these small, remote villages. There was no good or bad in it, but I had a choice to make. It now appeared that the teachings would be given in exchange for supporting their cause. Perhaps, the original message had not been so direct as the one that was delivered, but nonetheless, that was the message I heard. I could see it up ahead: the river was heading into a Y.

Until that time, I'd felt that my personal purpose and the council's purpose were the same: to bring the teachings and practice of these ways to the people here in the States. Practicing these ways with my sisters in the council was an added benefit. For me personally, it felt good to support the "cause" from a distance. After all, the culture and language were completely foreign to me, and what "they" need most from people outside their culture is money that is correctly funneled into the hands of those who will do the most good on the level of the human spirit and Mother Earth. It was a good cause, and one that I could support, but it was not my cause or purpose.

Seeing a Bigger Picture

That's the way I looked at it. I had reached the peak of the Medicine Shield, the North, and I was able to lift off on the wings of the eagle and see through its eye. With that vision, I could finally see a bigger picture. I could see that all the mountain streams merge with the rivers, and then they merge into the seas and oceans of the world. The North is the place where we realize the wisdom behind making choices in our life with a bigger picture in mind.

But, of course, I am not describing a physical hike up a mountain; this is an energetic, conscious hike. The North is about discovering the wisdom of that which we are, after we strip away everything that we are not. Imagine that you start this journey on flat ground with a backpack full of personal concerns and your self-importance. After a short while, the mountain that was once only a distant view is now under your feet. The path narrows and gets steeper. That is when you begin to feel your load getting heavier. Eventually, it becomes too heavy, and if you wish to continue one more step upward and forward, you will be forced to surrender a personal concern.

Our concerns and self-importance cloud who we are as a human consciousness, and everyone has to deal with these distractions of personality and daily life on various levels. The Vision Quest and the Hole experience had forced the wild mind to burn out in a matter of hours simply by putting the body/mind/personality into a situation were it had no distractions. The shield didn't work as quickly as the Hole, because I had to work with it in my daily life. I still had to live and work in the world while walking this path, which reminded me of the Herman teachings. He had told me: "Your work is now your yoga."

Here, I need to add a little more about the time the Shaman stayed in my studio. During the winter visit, she had become interested in renting the studio for a year with the idea of visiting multiple times. There had also been a decision to offer workshops in May of 2003. In other words, the council was busy and the current was moving swiftly enough that I had to pay attention.

Speaking my mind to the council was the peak of my experience in the North sector of the Medicine Shield. Shortly afterwards, I was well on my way to the circle of chiefs in the Northwest sector. These chiefs were with me before the shield was conceived. I painted them on the shield to acknowledge their guidance in the creating and unfolding this shield. The passage through the chiefs was all blessings and rejuvenation and a confirmation that all was well.

It had taken all of four years for me to travel through the five directions of my shield, starting in the South, when I first climbed upon the turtle's back. I then moved on to the eight-door teepee, the elk, the council circle, and the eagle vision in the North. Now, in a matter of a few weeks, I had passed through the circle of chiefs and was well on my way to the West, where I had painted the warrior's flying horse.

During this time, I had a communication with the Shaman concerning my shield. She had always had a keen awareness of where I was in the shield, so this communication was not unusual. Now that I was in the West, which was the seventh of the eight directions, the subject came up as to how things might unfold during the last phases of the shield. Until that point, it had always been obvious which direction would be the next. She suggested that I not bother with the Southwest circle of my shield and instead move directly into the center of the shield from the West.

At this point, it had been thirty-two years since I passed under the bridge that had confined my childhood and into the unknown. The purpose of the shield was to help me in meeting my Self. The West is also the direction where we tap into the conscious energies of intuition and discernment. These energies also happened to be the final two elements needed in the balancing of the shield. Thus, the Shaman's suggestion that I forget the Southwest section of my shield didn't sit well. Internally, the spirits of intuition and discernment started to raise issues about bypassing the Southwest. Eventually, I reached the conclusion that I needed to visit the circle and retrieve the dreams there before entering the center. The dreams were like creative seeds to be planted in Mother Earth sometime in the future. How and when they might sprout was not a concern.

I returned to the West. The West is about dreaming the dreams we hold within ourselves, knowing that whatever they may be will manifest in one way or another. It is serious medicine and not to be taken lightly. I felt, and still feel, nothing but gratitude for the Shaman's guidance in getting me as far as she had. But how else do we truly learn unless we eventually go it alone?

Intuition and discernment are highlighted in the West of the shield, but we should never forget the trust, clarity, and wisdom of the other directions. At a certain point, everything meshes and we need to be sure that the dream we are dreaming is our dream and that we are not being manipulated to fulfill someone else's dream.

As with the conflict over the "council's purpose," the idea of avoiding the Southwest circle of my shield to go directly to the center didn't feel right. Admittedly, and not on purpose, I had kept the Southwest a bit of a mystery. Until the day I buried it, I did not paint the inner images of musical notes, a book to be written, and a painted piece of art on the shield until the day I buried it. In fact, I did not paint the images until after I had pulled the boat to the lake and driven it across the water to the remote area. Only then, after I had tied off the boat, did I paint the final images.

Interestingly, it was the Southwest section of the shield that was most altered by Mother Earth during its six months' burial. Before I buried the shield, I was told that everything on the shield was "in play," and that this included how Mother Earth would affect the shield during its burial. It was all part of the magic and seriousness of creating a shield. The guidance I had received was impeccable.

Now it was the spring of 2003. Plans were being made and fliers were going out to the public for the upcoming seminars. Susan from the East Coast had planned to visit Taos and would camp in the backyard. Everything appeared to be running smoothly, as the river was fast and wide. Then, my daughter Jessica called from her school in Arizona and asked if she could live in my studio for the summer.

There was never a question in my mind, so I said, "Of course." The only problem was that I had to tell the Shaman that she could not rent my studio until September when my daughter returned to school. This didn't go over very well. She thought I should give her the studio instead of giving it to my almost-grown-up daughter. She was very clear, and I was very clear.

Ending My Time with the Shaman

During the next council meeting, the younger sister who had recently returned from Chiapas attempted to run the meeting. The Shaman had told her that she was to lead and that we were not to discuss these hot issues until the Shaman visited Taos in the middle of the following month. Of course, that would not be. The battle lines had been drawn before the meeting. It was our council. It was a good moment for everyone to speak from their hearts and minds. I told my story. There were other stories as everyone took the opportunity to speak.

Afterwards, I voiced that I was finished with the Shaman and had no interest in having the workshops at my house. Everyone but the young apprentice and the sister presently in Chiapas came to the same conclusion.

The sudden shift of the workshops from my house to another council member's home fifty miles to the southeast was a relief. At the same time, it presented an interesting situation. My council sister from the East Coast had planned to attend the Taos workshops and sleep in a tent in my backyard. Now that things had changed, she was told not to contact me, but this was unknown to me at the time. Apparently, I had lost my way and was "confused."

Grandmother: A Crystal Medicine Woman

By pure luck, on the day following our previous council meeting, I saw a poster at the local bookstore. A crystal Medicine Woman was offering private sessions. I decided that I should make an appointment, just to see what she might have to say about my situation. The crystal Medicine Woman was a wise grandmother type, and it was easy to feel her warm embrace. I had brought a few gifts, and Grandmother seemed pleased that I understood how to respect a medicine woman. We entered the session and moved easily through my questions.

When I spoke to her about my communication with my inner circle of chiefs in my shield's Northwest sector, she suggested that I no longer contact them and instead find the way myself. She followed with advice on how to cleanse and strengthen my energetic and physical body. After that, she gave me the blessing to continue to lead sweat lodges if I should choose to do so.

Grandmother communicated everything with her eyes closed and her hands on the crystal. Near the end of the session, I had one more question: "When will I meet my woman?"

After a moment, she lifted one hand off the crystal, palm upward, and said, "The bird you let fly away will return."

I didn't understand what she meant by "the bird," so I asked, "When would this be?"

Both of her hands were on the crystal again, and her eyes remained closed. She said, "Continue the practice I gave you for forty-five days."

More Intrigue

A few days before the mid-May seminars, Susan from the northeast called and informed me for the first time that she had been forbidden to contact me while visiting New Mexico. As I remember it, she was troubled about the abrupt change in the council and wasn't easily buying into the "Don't interact with Michael" storyline. She was my sister who had trusted me to take her to a remote place for her Vision Quest. Now, she had a choice similar to the one I'd had to make about my daughter staying at my place.

She arrived at my house the day before the workshops were to begin. This happened to also be the day before my buddy, Mark, and I were leaving for a three-day remote boat-camping trip.

Together, through our ability to share our perspectives and our experiences with the Shaman and the councils, we were able to piece together a bigger picture. Yes, there had been manipulation by the Shaman. I had learned from my council sister that the Shaman had discussed with her the possibility that she and I might one day get together in a relationship if everything worked out a certain way. I was not surprised to hear this. The pieces of the puzzle were coming together, and both of us could see a clearer picture.

We talked long into the night, and by morning, we were both paying the price for getting only a few hours sleep. I was heading off to go camping, while she was off to face the Shaman after disobeying orders. The new gathering place for the workshops was in a town that Mark and I would pass through on the way to the lake. We followed each other and had breakfast together in that town before parting ways.

Concha Lake was another seventy miles to the southeast and 2,100 feet lower in elevation. We planned to camp for three nights. Often during these trips, we'd grab our daypacks, a dozen golf balls, and a 9 iron, and go for long walks on the high desert mesa to practice our approach shots.

On this hike, I was leading the way from our camp on the lakeshore up along a narrow animal trail to the top of the mesa where we could practice. About halfway to the top, I looked down and saw that my left foot was about to step on a large sleeping rattlesnake. Startled, I jumped with my right leg to the right. Luck was with me, the rattler went to the left and immediately coiled, a rattle sounding its warning. Mark thought I had been bit. Not quite, but my heart rate was high, and I had no doubt that I had strained my jumping leg. It took hours for me to calm down.

In snake country, I had learned to walk slowly and to keep my eyes keenly focused on the ground a few steps ahead of where I would actually plant my foot. I used the same focus to reach down and pick up a stick for the fire. In reflection, it was after this episode of almost stepping on the rattler that my shield journey had closure. The counter-clockwise facing snake that originally determined the direction I would travel around the shield grabbed hold of its tail in its mouth and swallowed, and the shield no longer had a beginning or end.

A few days later, Mark and I were sipping our morning coffee and slowly packing up camp. Little did I know that Susan was on her way to the camp. She had been having a most difficult time at the seminar. On this same morning, she had decided to pack her things early and get out before seeing or talking to anyone, and she was driving to the lake to find me. She didn't know how she would find us since our cell phones didn't work, but she set off, anyway. In the meantime, Mark and I loaded the boat with our gear, drove across the lake, put the boat on the trailer, and headed home.

Now, there is no traffic in this area. It is possible to drive fifty miles and see no other car, and if you do, you usually pass each other at fifty or sixty mph. Susan had to drive seventy miles to get to the lake. There is only one place where the road is so narrow that I always stop my truck to let the approaching car or truck pass. This spot is on the narrow road that cuts across the Concha Lake Dam. On this morning, I stopped the truck to let a car pass, and it was Susan!

Back in Taos, we all decompressed for the next several days. We came to understand that, on some level, the Shaman had tried to manipulate events to help her cause. This we understood. We had no resentment; we had learned the warrior ways.

It was clear to me that the Shaman had been pulled deeper into her work with the Mayans. I was not to follow.

Deborah Reappears

The Medicine Shield story had played out over six years. It was now the middle of May in 2003, and for the first time in a very long time, everything was pleasantly calm and clear. I continued with Grandmother's instructions for the forty-five days, took care of my construction company, and hung out with my friend, Bryan Honda, the wild, crazy, and brilliant master of many talents.

On the forty-fifth day, Harry Belafonte was headlining at the Taos Solar Music Fest. There, the bird that Grandmother had said I let fly away reappeared. I thank the great spirits that I recognized Deborah completely before Harry stopped singing.

Michael Carroll

Chapter 12:
BODY WORK - THE ISSUE IS IN THE TISSUE

For all of my adult life, I'd had issues with my lower back, dating back to my pole-vaulting days and then compounded by the physical demands of construction work. I have a long list of healers and bodyworkers in my memory banks: the doctor who gave me my first spinal adjustment in high school, those who worked strictly with energetics, with or without light touch on certain points of my body, and then those who worked on deep tissue.

Of the deep-tissue workers, two stood out above the rest. The first was Douglas Blair, master bodyworker, teacher, and healer from Taos in the early 1990s. Douglas was the first practitioner to dig so deeply into painful places within my musculature that I left my body because of the pain.

Note: In the traditional sense, we may think of a spiritual master leaving his body during meditation and consciously entering the astral or spiritual planes as depicted in the watercolor by Herman.

However, I do not mean it in that traditional sense in this instance. The out-of-body experience during a deep tissue session is similar to breathwork, as both can trigger vivid visual and emotional memories from the past.

When Douglas was working on me, I witnessed what was causing the pain at its root. It amazed me to realize that not all injuries to our muscle and bone structure come from direct, physical blows or strains; injury to the physical structure can easily develop from mental and emotional stress related to an abusive parent, friend, client, or boss etc. Somewhere in the past, all of us have said things like, "He is a pain in my ass," or "She is a pain in my neck." For some reason, certain people make us cringe and tighten up physically when we are in their presence or when we think about them. As I screamed and squirmed on the massage table, Douglas asked in the most straightforward manner: "Who is a pain in your ass, Michael?" In a flash, my consciousness jumped into an altered state. Boom! I was disconnected in consciousness from the physical pain and taken to the origin and source of the tension.

In this case, the muscle tension in my ass cheek was pulling my lower spine out of adjustment and causing much pain. And, from what I was clearly seeing, the root of my pain was connected to a client whose house I had been building. Damn, he really was a major pain in my ass!

It quickly became apparent that undergoing deep muscular realignment is not just for physical healing. The physical is intertwined with our emotional and mental consciousness. Somehow, we humans have the ability to store vivid memories in our physical bodies that can be revisited and released through both bodywork and breathwork. With this understanding, we can use this modality as a spiritual tool to help in our quest to become clearer channels for love's light.

Deep-Tissue Work with Bryan Honda

"The issue is in the tissue" is a statement made by my friend, deep-tissue bodyworker Bryan Honda a master martial artist of many styles who is believed to be a distant blood relative of Master Miyamoto Musashi, the author of The Book of Five Rings, written in 1645. Bryan had trained with Bruce Lee for several months before he started his Hollywood movie career, and was at the time of our first meeting the bodyworker for the Denver Broncos. Bryan was a doctor of chiropractic medicine; and one of the early students who studied deep-tissue bodywork with Ida Rolf, the creator of the bodywork method known as Rolfing.

In the fall of 2001, when it looked like I might possibly need surgery on my back, someone suggested that I make an appointment with Bryan.

Bryan worked on me twice, and each time I felt great relief. He told me I could call him any time I was in need, so one Sunday afternoon, after I had returned from visiting Michelle at college in Denver, my back was so tight and painful that I could not stand straight. That Sunday afternoon, I called Bryan, and within an hour, I was on the table and feeling relief. He worked magic. That day, I committed to be a once-a-week client. That would continue for the next ten years.

Isolating and Detaching from Pain

First, he told me that he would not do chiropractic adjustments to my spine because the muscles were all lopsided and stuck together. In other words, I was tight and overdeveloped on the right side, not only from being a righty, but also because I'd used my right arm and side for banging framing nails into wood for way too many years without balancing it out by banging nails with my left. The overly developed muscles on the right had pulled my spine out of alignment. It was Bryan's job to realign the muscle structure. My job was to follow his instructions and learn to isolate and detach from the pain when he started digging into and stretching my muscles.

Just like undergoing basic training in the military or learning the basics of river rafting, there are foundational principles that need to be in place before having advanced healing practices performed on you safely.

If I wanted to heal, I had to become an active participant in the process, which meant that I needed to learn how to deal with the pain he would inflict on my body as he broke up knots and separated muscles that had gotten stuck together with what he called a kind of "glue" that had formed on my musculature from head to toe as a result of excess lactic acid buildup. Everyone has sore spots. Run your hand up and down your leg, foot, back, or arm and you will find sore spots. They hurt for a reason. Babies don't have them, little kids don't have them, but at some point in our teens and twenties, we start to develop them. If we do not deal with them, they will only make things worse as we age. Bryan told me the sore spots were places where the blood cells get blocked, thereby stopping or slowing circulation, like a clog in a water pipe. Unblock the clog, and everything flows better; the muscles move more smoothly, which relieves the sore spots so that you experience less and less pain.

My body was tight everywhere. Bryan had to chisel me for a good six months before he could even think about adjusting my spine. The idea was to loosen up and shrink the right side while loosening up and developing the left side until both became equal in size and movement. I was directed to stop playing baseball unless I was willing to start batting lefty and pitching lefty after playing righty for my entire life. Even now, fifteen years later, I still feel the urge to play every spring.

So, we are working with the body on the one hand, and on the other, we are stimulating our consciousness by adjusting to the change in physical habit. Suddenly, when something that has been part of our lives for a very long time dies with little or no warning, there is a void to be filled. It would be several years before I discovered the sport of disc golf, which easily allows me to use both my left and right sides equally. In the meantime, my focus between weekly sessions was to stretch every day and especially after playing disc golf or doing a day of construction work.

As an active participant, I was to breathe properly, relax, and isolate the pain. The session was an hour and a half long, and much of that time I was dealing with pain levels of five to ten. A couple of times, I screamed so loudly that we got kicked out of the rented massage space. Eventually, we just used my house.

I had to learn how to breathe through the pain. Bryan often grabbed or pushed into a spot until I nearly jumped out of my skin and found it impossible to take a slow, deep breath. Without letting up, he would ask, "Why are your shoulders, arms, and neck all tightening up while the spot I am holding is your foot?"

Isolate the muscle, breathe, isolate, breathe.

Often, he would play the role of torturer. He would ask me to imagine being held captive by the enemy while he grabbed hold of a spot and refused to let go. When the pain reached levels nine, ten, and beyond, sometimes I would cry, not in tears but in my voice. I can remember whimpering, " Mommy, Mommy," like a mantra.

This was the beginning of a unique voice lessons. I was introduced to something similar to the music scale, DO-RE-MI, but the sound was RUB-BER-DUCK-KEE.

The new notes were to begin when the touch of the massage started to become uncomfortable. In other words, instead of squirming or screaming, I was to focus my attention on the breath while singing the sounds, RUB-BER-DUCK-KEE. I was to find and hold the note or notes that vibrated with the pain, like playing keys on the piano while trying to find which note vibrates to our voice. I know it's a little weird, but the sound of our voice is a vibration that can be used to increase or decrease tension, similar to the way the soundtrack of a movie thriller or joyful movie helps to alter the viewer's emotional and mental body. The singing made it possible to stay present in the pain, and thus it opened the door to go deeper.

Proper Breathing

We all know how physical exertion can take us to the place where we need to stop for a moment to catch our breath. But are we aware of our general breathing habits and how useful it is to practice breathing slowly and deeply?

Babies and animals belly-breathe when they are in a natural, mellow state. Adults in general are no longer belly-breathers, since life stress tends to cause chest-breathing. Bryan instructed me to find a nice rock that I could place comfortably on my belly while I lay flat on my back. The goal was to breathe the rock up and down without using muscles to push it up or let it down.

Try it. To begin, place a small object on your navel area. The object is to witness the rhythm of your belly-breath. Up and down, in and out, breathe rhythmically as a practice. Eventually, if you practice this daily, your breath will become deep and slow.

Martial Arts

When I was a kid, the closest thing to martial arts was Saturday night wrestling on Channel 5, and I had never given it much thought until the time I met Ray in Myrtle Beach. In 1985, I had become a white belt at the local taekwondo studio. Eleven years later, in the summer of 1996, I received my second-degree black belt. Shortly after that, my training ended when the Medicine Shield and the general reorientation of my life took front stage. I tell this story because it was part of the driving force behind asking Bryan if he would be willing to teach me martial arts. It was not until I'd had more than a hundred and fifty deep tissue sessions that he agreed.

Bryan told me that I was plenty fast enough with my punches and kicks, and that what I needed to learn was how to move slowly and fluidly.

The Way of No Way

Bryan and I decided to add an extra session a week, during which we would do martial arts training. Essentially, I became a white belt in a particular teaching that Bryan referred to as "The way of no way." To give proper credit, Bruce Lee was the originator and master of this teaching. Bryan simply adopted what he had learned from Bruce and added his own experience to create his unique teaching and healing methods.

There were no punches, kicks, or anything that resembled martial arts training. The teaching was focused on developing the ability to move slowly from one place to the next smoothly and most efficiently, and then to spread that smoothness out to the full range of movement: hands to the floor, hands to the sky, hands close to the body, hands as far out as they can reach, and everywhere in-between—slowly. In many ways, the movement resembles the flexibility of a small child.

Here is an example: On a few occasions, we did a session in the small steam room, which had always been a great place to loosen up muscles and work on sore spots. On this day, however, I was instructed to lie on the bench with my head facing the door and then move my body around the U-shaped bench until my head faced the door on the opposite side from where I had started. Doing this in the normal manner might take ten seconds. However, I was told to take one-half hour to move from one end to the other. The practice was to always be moving, but super-slowly, like a worm or a snail, and without jerky movements. It was completely opposite to other physical disciplines I had experienced. The practice of slow physical movement became a meditation. At the time, I was entering my early fifties and needed to adjust to no longer being youthful.

For the first time in thirty-five years, I had a void to fill. I no longer had a spiritual teacher nor the yearning to seek another. I was adjusting to Grandmother's advice to seek within my self.

Michael Carroll

Chapter 13:
UNIVERSAL LAW AND SOUL DEVELOPMENT

The Purpose of Spiritual Work

In all of our spiritual work, what exactly are we trying to achieve? In the simplest terms, we are attempting to make contact with our true Self, our soul, and our eternal consciousness while we are here in a physical body.

Our spiritual work is not something separate. It is interwoven among all the other threads that create the fabric of our existence on the mental, emotional, and physical levels. Ideally, it is woven into all aspects of us. It includes our relationship with our personal inner voice, then spreads out into all our interactions with family, friends, and coworkers, and then embraces people everywhere.

Our inner and outward actions are responsible for the boulders, stones, and pebbles we toss into the water that surrounds and affects ourselves and others, creating ripples on the naturally clear, calm lake of consciousness. Through proper, steady practice over the years, eventually we learn to maintain a calm mind and a loving heart. Yet, this does not mean we are finished with difficult situations. It simply means that we have gained some level of expertise in travelling the river of life. Indeed, we have gone under the bridge into the unknown and come to understand that our material-world experience flows continually into the unknown until it ends. This is why Jesus said, "It is better to store your treasures in Heaven, where the thieves and others can't take it away."

I use the words "proper, steady practice" because that is what hones our internal sword, our consciousness. The nature of our inner sword allows it to develop according to our thoughts, words, and deeds in the world and within us. The sword is double-edged. The use of one edge makes things more difficult, and the use of the other edge makes things easier in the long run. One edge takes us into darkness and the other takes us into light.

Basic honesty is a spiritual practice that helps to bring about the best result of our actions upon all affected. We can reflect on our relationships and dealings in the world, which we have moved into and out of in all their various forms, and ask, "On what note did that situation end?" If we are honest, we should be able to sense whether a situation has come to completion or has been left unresolved. In a calm and non-judgmental state of mind, we can witness the repercussions of our actions for better or worse as they spread out in all directions. We witness this in our individual lives, and we can then bear witness to the ripples and waves that governments and corporations cause to befall the Earth and its people.

Making a better world is much easier than the mentality of our culture would have us believe. The goodness starts manifesting when individual thinking comes to a certain realization and understanding that transcends belief. For example, when I walked in the vibrating light and I saw and felt the difference between the ripples created by fear and those created by love, that was an experience that transcended belief.

We now are now aware that while we are living in the world, we are simultaneously living in another world of consciousness. We can see it in how we develop a relationship with the part of our Self that we become when distractions are no longer grabbing hold of our senses. Thus, sitting in a silent room with nothing to do can be a difficult challenge and provides a good reason to begin a simple meditation practice.

Attuning to the Subtle Currents

Herman taught us how to move through every experience with gratitude. As inexperienced rafters, we have our first adventure on an easy river. In the relative calm of a smoothly flowing river, we learn to pay attention to the subtleties of the current. Similarly, in our daily interactions with the world around us, we can learn to notice the subtleties.

We can pay attention to subtle currents even in how we check out at the grocery store. Everything matters. The next hint we need on the path can happen while we are pumping gas or paying our bill at the hardware store. Gratitude for every experience helps keep our consciousness present enough in the moment to see and read the signs along the way.

For the personality, gratitude is a learned response. We practice it like beginner white belts at a martial arts studio. Then, after some number of years of practice, gratitude becomes a valuable talent that is mingled with the core of our being. Gratitude is a life jacket, always worn or on hand.

When I was studying the Herman teachings, practicing gratitude meant constantly working to put out the fires of fear and anger. Fanning the flames of anger because someone cuts us off on the road or tries to do us wrong is a choice. Fanning angry thoughts is like fanning gas fumes toward a fire—just a little closer, and poof! That's how we create karma when we could and should avoid it. It's a discipline we can learn, just as a master river-runner has learned over miles and years on the river to maneuver around the boulders.

Fear comes into play when we become aware that the river continues flowing under the bridge and do everything in our power to avoid going under it. It's avoidance. "I don't want to look in the closet. I don't want to go there." It is a fear born out of our ego's lack of soul connection. It is afraid of the conscious knowledge of its true Self. The fear arises from knowing that we will have to experience the death of our ego in order to overcome it. The bible speaks to this when it says in Matthew 16:25 "For whosoever will save his life shall lose it: and whosoever will lose his life for my sake shall find it."

In Carlos Castaneda's book, *The Teachings of Don Juan: A Yaqui Way of Knowledge*, it says that fear is the first natural enemy of man and clarity is second. Having conquered fear, its ripples and waves no long occupy the attention of the mind. It is with this new clarity that a man begins to accumulate personal power. This is our personal sword to develop and wield as we see fit. Power is or becomes a natural enemy due to the great temptation to use the dark edge of the sword for personal gain at the cost of another's hardship. Man's misuse of the dark edge is the greatest cause of misery on our planet Earth.

When we talk about spiritual matters, we often choose words that describe other realms of existence that are not visible to the human eye. Heaven, Nirvana, The Promised Land, and Immortality all describe worlds beyond the limits of our human body senses. As an example, the human eye can see only 3 percent of the known light spectrum; our physical, dense world is 90 percent empty space, and our ears certainly do not hear all the sounds there are to hear. This is how and why an owl can see in the dark and a wild animal can hear and smell things humans can't.

In other words, something or some entity, be it a guardian angel or a bad spirit, could be standing right beside us in a frequency that we can't see or hear, and we wouldn't know it unless we were sensitive enough to feel it. We all know this "other sense" to a greater or lesser degree if we have ever walked into a holy space that is vibrating with love and light or a dark space that gives us "the creeps."

Jesus was no fool when he told us to love our enemies. He could see the bigger picture and the tangled mess we are in as human souls. He knew that our karmic debt had become unbearable. At that time, humans in that part of the world lived in fear of the dark edge.

The story in the Bible (John 1:29) tells us that Jesus came to take away the sins of the world. Exactly how could he do such a thing? How could he undo all the sin, pain, and suffering that humans had caused each other over thousands of years? How could he tell us that we reap what we sow and then come along and wipe the slate clean as if it never mattered?

The answer is, he couldn't. Universal Laws are not like human laws that we can break and get away with or that can be disregarded by a judge. Christ, however, did have the ability to ease our heavy burden by spreading out our karmic payback debt over multiple lifetimes, similar to spreading a home mortgage out over thirty years in order to keep the payments affordable. Jesus extended our karmic debt for two thousand years.

Exactly how Christ pulled that off is not unknowable. He did say, "Ye shall do greater things than I." However, at that time, we were like grade school children trying to understand doctorate level math and science. Jesus is the guy without sin, and he is clearly directing us as to how to become free from sin.

Universal Law

What happens when we die? Where do we go? Where are our great-great-grandparents now that they are no longer occupying bodies? And where are all the souls that lived before Jesus and after Jesus? Who were they, and where are they now?

Those souls that lived in the past were you and I. In order to work off our past sins, we are continually being born and dying and being reborn and dying again through these difficult years since Christ. All of our hardships of disease and savage killing of each other over the years was part of Christ's karmic payback plan. During the time of Christ, it was said that mankind's karma had become a crushing burden to carry, making it almost impossible for humanity to move forward. This is how and why Jesus got his nickname, "the Savior."

Imagine a Roman soldier back in the days when a warrior would think nothing of taking aim and letting his arrow fly into the heart of a peasant working in the field just to test his new bow. By the time his life was over, how many people had he killed? How many notches were on his weapon? Perhaps the warriors liked killing little babies, or perhaps they just blindly followed orders when: "King Herod, seeing that he had been tricked by the wise men, became furious and sent his warriors to kill all the male children in Bethlehem and in all that region who were two years old or under, according to the time that he had ascertained from the wise men."

If we do indeed "reap what we sow," then a Roman soldier who killed fifty babies with his sword would have to experience a fate equal to the fifty killings, including the resulting emotional waves that crashed upon the families and communities because of such sins. And this kind of human behavior went on for how many years before and after Jesus walked the Earth?

Think ahead to the Dark Ages, when the infant mortality rate was so high that eight out of nine children died before they reached the age of five. Conceivably during these times, it was possible for one soul to have fifty or more lifetimes born into the misery of savage death and disease, and all within a hundred years. Experiences such as these were necessary to bring our karmic account into balance. In everything, there is a good thing if we look deeply enough.

How Does Universal Law Work?

As scientists explore the known levels in the light spectrum that exists beyond human sight, new agers and other spiritually inclined people are exploring the different planes or levels of consciousness. One of the most commonly known is the astral plane, which is present and all around us; in fact, if we were clairvoyant, we would be able see into it.

In the astral plane, we find our conscious mental and emotional Self before and after our physical-body experience. This plane includes the full range of human consciousness, from its lowest to its highest. The difference in consciousness is measured by the quality of the vibration/light/love. When we die, we don't go to heaven, hell, or someplace in between, we go to the exact place in which we "are," relative to the quality of our vibration within the astral plane. Individually, as humans, we are a soul with a mental and emotional body that is vibrating in the astral plane while we are on Earth, learning how to integrate into a human body that we know has a limited lifespan.

There are stories that address the lower, hellish levels of the astral plane and stories that address the higher levels of consciousness in the astral realm. The basic rule of thumb is this: once we commit to having a physical life, we are bound by universal cosmic law to fulfill our

Earth mission, which is to become conscious enough to free ourselves from the cycle of birth and death. It can be a very long process from our first birth to our last!

Soul Development and Reincarnation

How many lifetimes does it take to complete this journey? I've heard many numbers over the years, from hundreds to thousands. For our purposes here, let's assume that it takes 500 lifetimes to complete the cycle from an innocent baby who has had no experience living in the physical realm to a fully mature, master-level, enlightened soul in physical form.

The rules of the game are as Jesus stated: "You reap what you sow."

Going back to the year 10,000 BC, the Earth's population was 1 million. Five thousand years later, it was 5 million; and by the time Jesus came around, the world population had reached 300 million. Fifteen hundred years later, it increased to 450 - 500 million. Three hundred years later in 1807, the population had doubled to 1 billion and would double again over the next 120 years to 2 billion in 1927. Over the next 90 years until 2016, the world population increased to 5 billion, 200 million—for a grand total of 7.2 billion incarnated souls.

To bring this closer to home, in 1800, the population of the United States was 5 million; in 1900, it was 75 million; and in 2000, it was 300 million—and notice that our population represents less than 5 percent of the present world total. This explosion of population has forced billions of inexperienced human souls to incarnate prematurely into extremely difficult situations because of the human requirement to have a soul for every physical body that is born on Earth.

Animals are different from humans because they do not create karma. When an old dog dies, it simply fades back into what might be considered a group soul, like raindrops into a pond of dog energy. Humans, on the other hand, do not fade back into a group soul; they retain the individual vibration of their mental and emotional bodies on the astral plane.

As children, before we attend kindergarten, we need to learn from our parents how to talk, feed ourselves, and use the toilet. In soul lives, the equivalent would be the soul's first experience of entering into and leaving a physical body.

In present times, nearly half the world's population, or more than 3 billion people, live on less than $2.50 a day, and of those, more than 1.3 billion live on less than $1.25. More than one billion are children, and according to UNICEF, 22,000 of these children die each day due to poverty.

You can let your imagination take you back through time and see that, on the difficulty/suffering level, not much has changed. We in 2015 still have poor, war-torn countries like those in 100 BC. In other words, the third world existed then as it does now. The big difference now is the size of the population. Billions of souls live short lives that are confined within the walls of extreme poverty. In this atmosphere, except for the rare bird, there is almost no hope or chance of rising up in consciousness beyond the simple needs for food and shelter. And if everyone were to rise up, where would they go? Where is the space in this world culture to accommodate the education and expansion of opportunity for all the 7 billion and counting souls on Earth? Something has to give, eventually, to force our world leaders to address this elephant in the room.

The more lives (incarnations) we have, the more interactions we have with other souls, thus we are in the process of learning all there is to know about life in the physical spectrum. Our arbitrary 500 lifetimes can be divided into five levels, and, like the astral plane, the physical realm also covers the full spectrum of vibrations, from the lowest dark, nasty stuff to the light of pure love.

Our lessons are long and slow because that is the situation we created. In an ideal world filled with wisdom, the number of lifetimes needed to achieve mastery would be drastically fewer. Clearing the obstruction of darkness from our active minds and the planet is and will be the result of our spiritual work. In the extreme of the third-world jungle, however, the village focus is on survival, and this is based on the threat of starving to death or dying early from ill health.

Early Childhood Souls (The first hundred or so lifetimes)

In the third world, deep in the rural land of Chiapas, I visited a remote village where no white man had been before. As we walked into the village, all of the women, young girls, and small children stayed huddled inside the dark, wood-smoke-filled community kitchen shack.

We didn't stay long. As I remember, we were there on council business, dropping in with verbal communications because the village had no electricity, no cell phones, and no vehicles. This village, in my eyes, was about as low as we can go as humans and survive (as long as the weather doesn't get weird). What would be below this? Refugees starving on the roadside? These people had nothing, and the outside world paid them zero attention. It was luck that the council had made contact and was willing to offer assistance when the people were in the early stages of developing better ways to feed themselves. From my perspective, in comparison, the corn-water soup village was a model and a sign of progress.

After we got back in the car, I asked the Shaman what the people's power animals were. Most of the people had been a little afraid of us strangers. The Shaman said that the power animals of most of the villagers were the tiny animals in the forest: the mice, chipmunks, and so on. The power animal of the leader was a dog—no doubt, he was the rare one I spoke of earlier. He was obviously an older soul. How much older? It was hard to say, and I would like to note here that older souls always have the option to incarnate into a more difficult environment as a mission of service to humanity.

None of us gets to where we are without the help and guidance of others. In the case of the leader with the dog power animal, it was clear that his soul had incarnated into a difficult living condition with a mission to help bring a larger vision to the community. We can imagine how the loyalty of dog energy would be a perfect match in this particular situation. As a comparison, we can imagine a council leader being an eagle, able to grasp the bigger picture from above and also having the uncanny ability to also focus on the finer details playing out on the ground.

After a hundred lifetimes, give or take, we humans would have developed a simple mind and progressed enough emotionally that we would be ready to wholeheartedly start following a leader into the new and different territory outside of the core family/village influence.

Grade School Souls (the second hundred lifetimes or so)

During the next hundred lifetimes, we would have expanded on those basics. Our mind, emotion, and consciousness would have developed to a stage similar to that of a grade school child. During those developmental years, we would have absorbed what we were taught without question. We would have followed blindly, because at that stage, we knew nothing of the bigger world around us and were completely dependent on those who appeared to guide us: mother father, priest, teacher, political leader, or public figure.

People at this stage in the cycle of development are those who are quite happy and content working at jobs, especially jobs that require a low level of responsibility. I met some of these simple-minded guys in the army. Most, if not all, came from rural places, and I readily noticed that they did not question much, if anything, about what they were being told to do.

Of course, older souls work these kinds of jobs, as well, but I am trying to make a little order out of this confusing and often avoided subject, so I will set that aside. The uncomplicated souls I am speaking of do not cause the wars, but they are most often the ones on the front line for country or king.

Another example of an experience available to a relatively inexperienced soul might be an incarnation as a poor, inner-city kid. It's not nice compared to the cushy American middle class in the last half of the last century. Yet, from another perspective, it is a life of luxury compared to the Dark Ages.

The soul born into the ghetto faces a completely different and more complex environment. In the ghetto, life is about learning how to get along with other humans inside the concrete jungle where Mother Nature is virtually non-existent. In the third world, we learned how to live on the land and avoid the poisonous snakes and bugs; in the ghetto, we learn how to develop the ability to communicate and defend, not only physically, but also mentally and emotionally. Remember, we are always in the process of developing our sword, and great lessons are learned in difficult situations. Getting through rough, turbulent waters without getting flipped off your raft is a major accomplishment for any soul of any age.

The ghetto is not all bad from that perspective, because the present nature of our world requires that we learn how to toughen up on all levels. Being nice and sweet is fine in the right place and at the right time. Toughening up has something to do with knowing and feeling the correct line to take when your raft enters turbulent waters. Boulders are everywhere, and you discover it is wise not to travel in the dark. Millions—or I should say billions—of souls presently live in ghettos across the world. Most of them are good human souls who are learning to do the very best they can in a difficult situation.

Teenage Souls (the third hundred lifetimes or so)

Blindly killing the enemy for a power-hungry, corporate country or king creates individual karma for the warriors and for the power-hungry souls manipulating the world stage. And it is within this stage of the developmental cycle, after two hundred or more lifetimes, where most of the human trouble arises. Here, if not properly guided, it is easy for the soul to get tangled up in selfish ego power. This stage of lifetime soul experience can be compared to newly sexually awakened people in their early teens and on into their twenties. It is a time of experimentation and a grab for personal power. Our desires are inflated. The danger is highlighted when we want something badly enough that we pull our sword from its sheath and cut with the dark edge in order to take it. It is when, for personal gain, we become willing and active participants in making things more difficult for others to safely float downstream. In the eyes of Universal Law, we are responsible for the shipwrecks we cause through the selfish obstacles we create. The individual or CEO who knowingly dumps toxic substances into a river to save money may presently live a wealthy life as a person of status, but has he listened to Jesus' words of wisdom when he spoke about where to store our treasures?

We can assume that the phrase, "He sold his soul to the devil," applies to a teenage soul willing to use the dark edge of the sword to speed ahead, having little or no concern for the repercussions. We can see this clearly in the world of corporate business and politics.

Our culture promotes competitiveness throughout the educational years. Then, we are expected to transition into young adulthood. However, what if the soul personality in the body is not yet ready to mature? What if the personality's inflated desires continue to grow more powerful? What if, instead of becoming responsible young adults, we remain focused on selfish dreams because we adopt the win-at-all-costs mentality? The simple reality is that this is the stage of soul development in which the temptation to do something sneaky is most prevalent. The natural consequence for such behavior is the creation of karma.

When winning at all costs leads to doing something dirty and unethical, we can be sure that we have a bad case of "wanting," and we can be sure, too, that there will be a price to pay when it all catches up. A little pollution dumped into a river can be absorbed and transformed, and the river can be restored to its natural vitality, just as our bodies can recover from an overdose of wine or beer at a Saturday night party. Do it again the next night and the next, and eventually there will be a breakdown.

This is what can happen when people do not grow beyond the mental attitude of a teenage soul. They are the CEOs and lobbyists who buy senators and congressmen, putting corporate interests over human interests.

Teenage Souls and the Manifestation of Desires

As my LSD experience with the energy of the waves illustrates, whatever we think affects the quality of vibrations on the astral plane. It matters not that we don't see or feel it, as it still exists just outside of our perception. It works like this: we think and desire something in our minds first, then, as we visualize and remain focused, eventually our desire manifests into our physical reality. Again, it is the use of our free will that determines which edge of the sword we use in seeking our dream, and the law of karma is what brings about the eventual result of the action. An unwise or inexperienced soul, due to its lack of experience, forgets or never considers the next life.

If we are wild, teenage souls, we may have little empathy for the loser and not care about the ripple effect we have caused in the world. Every parent of a wild teenager knows what I am talking about. All we have to do now is shift our perception from physical age to soul age to grasp the mentality of those running the show on the world stage.

What kind of soul mentality did our leaders have when they decided to kill the Native Americans as they traveled westward in search of their dreams? Lead bullets allowed the soldiers to fire upon the Indians from a distance beyond which their arrows could fly. Reflecting, the Indian Wars took place between 1817 and 1898. The United States deployed 106 thousand servicemen over those years and suffered a thousand soldier deaths, while the Indians over that same period suffered somewhere in the range of 10 million deaths. What has changed over the years? We've had one war after another, all the while being told that we are the greatest country in the world without doing the research as to which edge of the sword the leaders of our culture used to get us into our present situation.

There is a reason why the United States prospered so nicely after World War II. It was because our manufacturing competition around the world had to recover from the destruction. However, by the late Seventies, the world's playing field, perhaps for the first time in history, had become competitive.

Advanced Souls (the fourth and fifth hundred lifetimes or so)

The reason the Vietnam anti-war movement had such an impact upon our culture was mostly due to the influx of older souls who had incarnated into the United States and other first-world countries on a massive scale just before and after World War II. Astrologically speaking, by 1953, Earth had moved into the Age of Aquarius, the time of enlightenment. By the mid-Sixties, these older, more experienced, souls started to reach their late teens and early twenties in physical age. This was when the first major wave of souls whose total life experiences numbered in the 300 - 400 range made their presence felt in the fabric of our world.

Naturally, these older souls clearly could see beyond the bully tactics of the government, and they spoke out against its assumed authority that deceived the people into the Vietnam War. It was a war that killed 58,000 Americans and an estimated 4 million Vietnamese, a statistic that does not include the physically and mentally wounded.

Eventually, no matter whether we came here as brand-new souls, child souls, teenage souls, or advanced souls, our blinders begin to admit more light and, at the level appropriate to our soul's experience, we take up the quest to find our true Self.

At some point, the personality realizes and can no longer deny that something more exists that is beyond the normal 3 percent we see and feel with our senses. It is both a painful and a blissful realization for the ego that, after having spent years/lifetimes selfishly fixated on winning a game in what now they realize was a drastically limited arena.

Upon that realization, for the first time in our awareness, we understand how small we are in consciousness relative to the unknown and reach out from a very deep place to say, "God help me!" so that we can begin the long walk back home. Finally, after creating a lot of karma, we recognize that it is time to start disciplining our selves to use the light edge of the sword.

As young adults can see earlier folly, so too do teenage souls grow to see the foolishness of the actions inspired by their teenage minds and, becoming young adult souls, can begin the process of swinging back over the way we came in order to witness, and somehow help to correct, the destruction we may have left behind us. How many lifetimes does it take to swing back across the path we created to correct the results of our actions when we were teenage souls? That depends on what we did during those lifetimes.

Most who refused the draft were not the cowards that our "teenage" leaders assumed they were. The media, too, portrayed us as cowards that needed to be absorbed into our cultural belief system. These men, including me, were not afraid to die; they simply knew from a deep place within that they didn't want to be involved in the killing. In some ways, it takes more courage and conviction to stand up and live by our beliefs than it does to follow orders for the mass killing of a declared enemy of our country or king. There is nothing wrong with self-defense when we are attacked, however there is something wrong when the high school bully and his gang pick on the grade school kids and deprive them of enjoyable experiences.

The war machine loves money and power as it dreams of ways to control people with military force. It feeds the evil forces that are willing to fight, just as surely as a junkie seeks his next fix. Those who are part of the war machine are like teenagers playing Monopoly on the world stage. We can call them ruthless motherfuckers because that is what they are. They are also our brothers and sisters who are willing to stop at nothing and to do everything conceivable to get what they want. They are the tidal waves on the ocean of life.

In our present period of mass communication, we the people are no longer limited to receiving one-sided, spoon-fed news stories from the mainstream media. Leaders with teenage souls have abused the dark edge by controlling information and in some cases enforcing hellish rules the people must live by. Over the years, we became accustomed to and/or witnessed abuse on all three levels—physical, emotional, and mental—and we had little or no ability to break free from it until now.

The flow on the information highway presently moves unrestricted and invisible through the airwaves, and it is penetrating the normally solid walls that enclose our normal 3 percent of awareness. As we enter day by day and year by year into the age of enlightenment, this new, free-flowing information within the realm of human communication is bringing us one step closer to uncovering Earth's sneaky, dark underworld.

Even more important, for the first time since before the great flood, Earth's first world is populated by large numbers of incarnated, older souls, and they have zero interest in taking advantage of people simply because they can. Without getting too religious about it, I can say that these souls naturally understand the wisdom in the words: "Do unto others as you would have others do unto you." At this stage, there is a new knowing on a gut level that it is better not to make unnecessary waves now that the inward journey has begun.

Let's also keep in mind that, as I write this in 2016, many world leaders still have but one interest, and that is to prevent people from, as I have been putting it in this book, "going under the bridge and into the unknown." They speak not of improving the entire world, but only their own.

They will fight on any and all levels to get what they want. The spraying of Agent Orange, which eventually killed bodyworker Bryan Honda, was a major sin that one nation committed upon another. A big country like the U.S. sent millions of men to fight in the jungles of a country that is only a thousand miles long and forty miles wide. We also gave blankets covered with smallpox virus to the Indians on purpose, so I can only imagine how sneaky things have gotten during our present wave of modern technology.

Now, with the worldwide internet, we have truthful information available to us if we are willing research and discern the light from the dark. However, our government and the corporate powers often wield the dark edge; they censor what we hear just as a mother determines what her child will eat during the transition from breast milk to solid foods. Just stop and think about it. Six corporations control all two hundred fifty media outlets that serve over three hundred million people in our country alone. Think back to how both presidents Johnson and Bush lied the people into war by using the news media outlets. Johnson lied to one hundred ninety million people, and Bush lied to two hundred and eighty million. Following both lies, our country started an aggressive war.

However, the new wave of mass online communication makes it possible for people to hear another side of the "official story," something never before possible.

The government's answers to and reasons for the free-fall collapse of the World Trade Center were presented to the American people by an independent, bipartisan commission that was chartered to prepare a full and complete account of the circumstances surrounding the terrorist attacks in the same manner as did the Kennedy assassination's Warren Commission. We may never know the full story behind the Kennedy assassination, but I do believe that the twenty-seven pages blacked out on the 911 Commission's report to Congress will eventually shine some light into the darkness.

At some point, the young adult in us finally figures out that, yes, it's good to work hard and get what you want, but there is long-term value in the wisdom of wanting a good deal for all concerned. Screwing others to get ahead no longer feels justifiable internally because we have begun to understand and feel how emotions and thoughts are intertwined. A teenager's strong willpower can temporarily cut off the emotional feeling nature and turn parts of the mind into ice. In the extreme, we refer to incarnated souls at that level as cold-hearted bastards.

Developing and maintaining honesty changes everything. The fighting and bickering around the world can finally settle down once we elect leaders who begin by thinking in terms of what is best for all concerned. This shift has been made especially difficult in part due to our powerful U.S. government culture that continues to tell its citizens (who represent just 4.5 percent of the world's population) that they are the greatest in the world. Perhaps that was true for a brief time, but that time has passed. American exceptionalism contains fragments of the BS from Catholic Church teachings, which taught us from the time we were children that we were the only ones who would get into heaven.

Contrary as it may sound, the willingness to "become as little children" is a necessary next step in our soul development. It is surrendering into the unknown, ever so lightly, for the first time. You know how it is. Life is great, and then you get hit with a wave that simply stuns your mind and takes your consciousness to a new place where you have the opportunity to sense new depths in your awareness. Perhaps for the first time we may be able to appreciate that, generally, there is a good reason for getting whacked upside the head. Perhaps our old reaction, which was to punch back immediately, no longer holds power over our decision-making process. This is a huge swing in awareness.

We have started training to no longer blindly wield the dark edge of the sword and have begun the process of seeking to do "good works." We are swinging back across the path we created as teenagers with the purpose of righting all our wrongs and meeting up with our friends.

These are now the young adults we see around us—friends from past lives who were our lovers, sons, daughters, mothers, and fathers.

Remembering that sin is the eventual result of our actions, we need take into consideration the ripple effect of our actions upon others as it moves outward physically, mentally, and emotionally across the population. This is why we have been given the Golden Rule: "Do onto others as you would have others do unto you."

This place in time is where the tide is just beginning to shift. No one really knows exactly how it will work out, but we can be sure that the souls who have never considered that the tide might one day turn will freak out and do their best to resist facing their Self and all they have done. This drama is now playing out on the world stage and within our daily lives.

For the first time, the power structure of the world leaders is cracking. How long will it take us to hit the Wall of Dreams and be forced, as a mass consciousness, to accept that the tide is turning to the East sector of the Medicine Wheel so that we can gain a little clarity on our situation? Using 1940 as a starting date, it has taken seventy-six years to get this far, and in another twenty-four years, it will be a hundred years. By then, more advanced souls will have infiltrated the population in greater numbers that include all living generations. In other words, this is still only the beginning of a major shift in consciousness on the planet.

Yes, we have been tricked and fooled, much as freshmen are abused by the students above them. But now, for the first time in perhaps thousands of years, there are enough young adult and elder souls among the population to see through the bullshit and begin the process of dismantling the power of selfish leaders.

We have to be willing to stand up and speak our truth, just as young Private Carroll did: "I don't believe in killing people, Drill Sergeant." And yes, I can attest that it does become much easier to speak your truth when you have a group of like-minded souls who embrace the same higher concept.

Things are different now as I write this book. Increasingly more souls are becoming aware that we are not limited by the materialism of the normal 3 percent of human awareness. We are beginning to realize the importance of mental and emotional stability as we see larger sections of the population struggling in areas that are outside of our physicality, such as mental and emotional instability, which is reflected in the increasing use of antidepressants to ease our troubled thoughts. I think we can all agree that the mental health of humanity is not in the best condition.

Here is a quote from Autobiography of a Yogi, by Paramahansa Yogananda, who founded a spiritual school in the U.S. in the last century:

> Don't depend on death to liberate you from your imperfections. You are exactly the same after death as you were before. Nothing changes; you only give up the body. If you are a thief, a liar, or a cheater before death, you don't become an angel merely by dying. If such were possible, then let us all go and jump in the ocean now and become angels at once! Whatever you have made of yourself thus far, so will you be hereafter. And when you reincarnate, you will bring that same nature with you. To change, you have to make the effort. This world is the place to do it.

Herman referred to death as "crossing the rainbow bridge," the bridge of many colors that takes us from the darkness of the 3 percent of awareness and places us directly back into the astral plane of eternal light and vibration. As Yogananda said, nothing changes in relationship to your vibration. You are still your individual consciousness of mind/feeling/soul, but minus the human animal we use to experience Earth life.

Obviously, those evil bastards who caused such misery will not find themselves in the same place as the kind-hearted. However, as good people, we are greeted upon our crossing of the rainbow bridge by old family, friends, angels, holy beings, and teachers. The teachers are generally wise old human souls who have learned all the lessons within the 3 percent of normal human awareness and have advanced beyond the need to incarnate. Yet, they are humans just like you and I, and they are referred to in the Bible as, "Those who are first will be last." They are the captains of the ship who make sure everyone is aboard before we take off into the next realm.

These wise masters are the ones who help us understand and absorb the lessons contained within the physical life we have left behind and prepare us for our next incarnation. In human time, the next incarnation could be as soon as a matter of days, or it could be hundreds or even thousands of years from now.

What we have learned, and what we need to learn in preparation to meet our next life purpose, is unique to everyone. That is another reason that we ought not to judge other people's soul purpose within their present life. We all observe the world and choose our course of action. In that way, we are like river runners who observe the currents they are facing and choose our path forward as we see fit.

What makes the difference between a river guide and someone else is experience on the river, clarity of mind, and oneness with the body. How well the body and mind work together is directly related to the oarsman skill.

When an older soul is born, that soul still acts his physical and emotional age as a baby, a pre-teen, a teenager, and a young adult as he moves through each of these physical-age stages. What we become and what we do once we reach the physical age of adulthood has everything to do with our individual soul mentality/consciousness. As the saying goes, "It's what's on the inside that matters." An elder soul matures and becomes wiser with physical age, while a younger soul continues to wildly wield the dark edge of the sword for selfish gain.

Another way to view our Earth life is from the perspective of "soul purpose" for a particular incarnation. As an example, on the extreme end of the spectrum of human development we have Jesus, who grew up as the oldest son of Mary in a family that included six younger brothers and sisters. We can assume that Jesus' purpose was to become the channel for the Christ sometime around his physical age of thirty-three. What happened during the first thirty-three years is revealed in the Book of Enoch. The point is this: our soul's purpose and our daily work to support a family are often two different things. Jesus the carpenter actually developed a construction company during his day to support his mother and younger siblings. As the boys grew up, they naturally became carpenters under Jesus' supervision. During these years, Jesus continued running the business as he took time off to study with the area's religious teachers. By the time Jesus was in his later twenties, his brothers had the business well in hand, and so Jesus was able to travel for extended periods to places as far away as India so he could visit with the spiritual masters of the time.

Was it Jesus' soul purpose to be a carpenter or to be a channel for the Christ? Everyone needs to do something in the 3 percent material world to support their life. Chop wood, carry water, weed the garden, clean the house, keep accounts, and so on. He chopped wood, but being a carpenter was not his life's purpose. Chopping wood and gardening could very well be the purpose for a person who was a baby soul in the village.

In the astral plane, we all get exactly what we need to prepare for our next birth. We work this out with our guides on the astral plane before our mothers give birth to us. To help us fulfill our purpose, we make plans with other souls to meet up somewhere along the way. None of our close friends and major experiences is accidental.

Yogananda said, "Everything depends upon the quality of our personal vibrations." I've read stories of both hellish and heavenly places within the astral plane. Imagine a severe alcoholic dying and finding himself in an out-of-body experience in some funky bar. His alcoholism was so severe that his personality was unable to leave the attachment to alcohol even upon leaving the body, so the 3 percent, bodiless mental and emotional structures of the personality wind up in some funky bar, gasping for a drink but unable to satisfy the craving because, although he can see everything in the 3 percent world, he no longer has a physical body.

When you walk into a bar and get a creepy feeling, you might safely assume that one or more of these astral entities are hanging around. They are addicted to an obsessive desire and can't let go of it. The same thing can happen with extremely violent personalities. They can end up in the lower astral world—the pits of hell—where their sick acts of violence in the 3 percent world play out endlessly against other souls of similar fate. Nothing much changes for them, except now they are in an astral energy body on the astral pane 24/7.

Although these souls are in what is considered the pits of hell, there is a way out through the angels of mercy, who, by and through their love, watch over the suffering, drunken, fighting souls with open arms, as we see painted on cathedral ceilings. All the struggling soul needs to do is look up, reach out, and call, "God help me!" It's that simple.

Back in their physical body days, many of these souls were what we call possessed. It's a "The devil made him do it" kind of thing. This is because our thoughts, while we are in the physical world hold that exact quality of energy. For example, imagine the thoughts of Saint Francis caring for the sick and compare them to the thoughts in the mind of a soldier killing babies with his sword and then raping the mother.

What we think in the 3 percent attracts to us the qualities of that same vibration on the astral plane. When we imagine and focus our thoughts on the ideas we wish to manifest in the 3 percent, we attract entities around us of a similar quality. A thief attracts thieving souls, and a saint attracts saintly souls. When a goodhearted soul seeks understanding of the way to get back to the Great Spirit, she attracts to herself entities of a finer, more spiritual, vibration to help them along the inward way. It is the same for artists of all kinds. In other words, we are not alone, and we attract to ourselves exactly what we think, feel, and pay attention to.

Hell will be around as long as humans need it to be there, but there will come a time when the greater part of humanity will be ready to move its home base on the astral plane to the next level, which I will call the soul plane. Exactly when this will happen is debatable, but there will come a time when there will be enough souls ready to cycle into the next realm of consciousness, and that will force a split, leaving behind certain members of the human race. The Bible talks about this when it refers to "Judgment Day."

On the soul plane, we are one with our "Self." We have completed our karma, aligned our three bodies, and have become pure channels for the soul. In essence, we have been enlightened, and we live in the 3 percent world only to serve the greater spiritual plan for humanity. We are indeed living, "on Earth as it is in heaven."

How long have we humans been on Earth, going through these cycles? How many Earth shifts have we experienced in which continents rise and fall since the time when the first souls entered human bodies? In actual Earth years, our scholars have estimated that humans have been around somewhere between 200,000 and 3.5 million years. This is hard to comprehend, as it makes our relatively known history over the last 13,000 years only a small drop in a vast ocean of time. Astrologically speaking, 13,000 years is only halfway through one cycle of the twelve signs of the zodiac, and only halfway around the photon belt. It is also the estimated time since the Earth's last major pole shift, referred to as "the great flood" in the Bible. Now, due to modern Earth science, we have developed some measure of understanding as to what happened back then.

Essentially, the Earth got whacked by a large object from space, and much of our land and water exchanged places. What had been the central spinning axis of our Earth shifted eighteen degrees. The molten liquid center core of the Earth was jarred to such an extent that it pushed up the Earth's crust in some areas, which caused sinking on the opposite side as that one to two thousand-plus degree inner Earth liquid responded to the impact. We should also keep in mind that the Earth is spinning at 1040 miles per hour on its axis, so no place was left unaffected. The Earths' crust continued to be altered for many years until, finally, the molten liquid stopped swaying, and the surface crust could settle down.

Then, a new Earth rhythm was set in motion. Not only did humanity have to start all over from scratch, we also had to deal with a new 365-day, four-season cycle. Prior to the flood and before the axis of the Earth shifted, everything was consistent. The rising and setting of the sun never changed. There were no seasons to move into or out of. In contrast, our present Earth's equator is the only place on Earth today that remains consistent, including no ocean tide.

The shift in the weather pattern was a major trauma for the survivors. Imagine how long it took to figure out the new 365-day cycle? How wildly more extreme could it have been? It turned into a nightmare as the Garden of Eden disappeared and our animal survival instinct rose to the surface. We had to become hunters and to protect ourselves with spears and arrows tipped with obsidian or stone points. We can imagine we were like the native Indians who lived on the land for thousands of years until less than two hundred years ago.

What now comes to mind are all the souls who lived on the Earth thousands of years ago on what have become known as the continents of Atlantis and Mu. Those souls, too, are part of our human family, and it is highly possible that many of us now alive lived in those times, as well. Imagine that then we were governed by elders wise on all levels, and that the teenagers, although still wild in nature, were raised in the wisdom and understanding of the way things are.

Taking our long past into account, we are able to see how there could be a huge population of young adults, elders, and masters among our human brotherhood and sisterhood who are consciously living on the astral plane, and who, because of the cataclysm, have rarely incarnated since. Yes, there have always been places for the older souls to incarnate around the world, but it was not until the 1930s and 1940s that the opportunity for mass incarnations became available due to the explosion in the population and the expansion of consciousness that would begin taking place as modern technology took root.

In the astral world, we experience the true meaning of 24/7, because it never gets dark, our bodies no longer need to eat or sleep, and everything is one with its own light. The astral world is eternal, we are eternal, God is eternal, and our eventual goal is to become fully conscious of our eternal soul consciousness while we are living in the 3 percent world.

If the stories passed down to us are correct, we have traveled around and through the twelve signs of the 26,000-year zodiac cycle at least seven times and perhaps for over a hundred cycles, depending on which stories we read. For example, Moses walked the Earth at the beginning of Aries (four thousand years ago). Some two thousand years later, when Jesus walked the Earth, we entered the Piscean Age. Pisces is the Latin word for fishes, and it has the two-fish symbol. It also happens to be one of the earliest zodiac signs on record, dating back to 2300 BC. Old souls in those days didn't have computers, but they did have highly developed minds that were able to track the movements of the heavens.

• • •

When will humanity learn its lessons and graduate to living full-time on the soul level?

The prophecy known as "Judgment Day" refers to the moment when the human consciousness will shift from being astral-based to soul-based, with the implied reality that some souls are simply not ready to graduate.

From what we have discussed, it's not hard to imagine who the souls are that might be left behind. There are some major, evil dudes buzzing around in the 3 percent who have zero desire to rise above selfishness and are continually willing to wield the dark edge upon others simply because they can.

In Luke 17:2, it says, "It were well for him if a millstone were hanged about his neck, and he were thrown into the sea, rather than that he should cause one of these little ones to stumble." Jesus was referring to the seriousness of the karmic debt we receive when we interfere with another soul's ability to progress, especially when we do it consciously and for selfish, personal gain. He is telling us to pay attention to the ripples we create upon the lake of life, the ones that we will be held accountable for either now or in the future. "Do unto others as you would have others do unto you," is a statement that reflects wisdom.

Again, the difference between a man and an animal is that the man is subject to the law of sin.

Christ had no sins, and he taught the path of no sins. The Christ showed us that "Love is the way," and he lived a life to prove just that point. Why attain the world only to lose it when the physical body is no longer available? Why get addicted and give all our attention to materialism when we know it is not available in the astral or soul worlds?

After approximately four hundred lifetimes, we become elders. We have been on both sides of just about every possible human experience. Yes, we still have karma, however it's no longer the heavy karma we may have incurred through the killing and major abuses we committed in an earlier life. We now align our lives with learning how to achieve balance in our human relations.

Elder souls are good people who are trying to the do the best they can with what they have. All situations test our ability as rafters on the river of life to read the currents and control our raft. We understand that we are attempting to get around or through turbulent situations without creating more turbulence for others. It is a sign of maturity when we realize that smacking someone over the head with an oar because we judged him to be an asshole is not a good thing to do. It is a realization that has repercussions. Forever after, we will strive to remember that everything is vibrating light just beyond the limits of our normal eyesight, and that, in reality, there is no place to hide.

The spiritual practice of purification for all three bodies is what allows us to continue cleansing the residue left over from our past experiences within our Self. This can be looked at as "self-Karma" as opposed to Karma with another soul.

This book is mostly about the 3 percent of awareness and the astral and the soul planes because we humans are presently making our way across or through the astral consciousness to the soul plane of consciousness while living in the physical. However, there are other known planes of consciousness beyond our soul level. In fact, our soul level is considered the bottom rung of the spiritual consciousness ladder.

In the Bible, when Jesus says, "Ye shall do greater things than I," he is speaking from the seventh level of consciousness. He is letting us know that there is a clear path to his level of awareness and beyond—if we choose to live by the code of ethics that he set forth.

The trust Jesus is asking us to realize when he says, "Seek first the kingdom of God and all else will be given," is exactly the same kind of trust we find in the South on the Medicine Wheel. There is no difference other than the method of getting there.

For humanity, there is no rush, and yet there is a timeline. There will come a time when the gap between those souls who are attuning to the higher spiritual vibrations and those who have created an overwhelmingly dark karmic debt will no longer be allowed to intermingle in the same world. That judgment will not be made by man, but by the lords of karma who reside in realms beyond our astral plane. The majority of all human souls on all levels—including teenage souls—are good people. Yes, we've all done our fair share of stupid stuff and have learned and moved on. But there are also the "evil bastards," those with a karmic debt so deep and heavy that when the day arrives for humanity to graduate, these souls will be left behind in their own reality with others of similar fate somewhere in the 3 percent universe until they wake up.

Michael Carroll

About the Author

In June 1972, at the tail end of the Vietnam War, Michael Carroll was drafted into the Army. Less than a year later, he was discharged, not because he was physically unfit but because a very loud voice inside his mind started telling him that he didn't want to be trained to kill.

Michael moved to Taos New Mexico in 1975, and for the next ten years became a disciple of a spiritual teacher. No money was charged, but there were rules: no drugs meat or alcohol and a daily meditation practice that focused on training the ego personality to love everyone without criticism.

In the late 1980s, Michael was introduced to the Native American path. The Medicine Wheel, a four-day vision quest, journeying on the sound of the drum, power animals, sweat lodges, and adventures in the Mayan lands of Chiapas, Mexico, were all part of his experience for the next fifteen years.

After more than forty years of actively seeking the Kingdom of God within, Michael shares his story and knowledge of our purpose as eternal souls living in physical bodies.

As a father of three daughters, Michael earned his living as a carpenter/general contractor, building homes in Taos, New Mexico. For fun, he camped, fished, played baseball, guitar and disc-golf, and studied martial arts.

www.ingramcontent.com/pod-product-compliance
Lightning Source LLC
Chambersburg PA
CBHW070609300426
44113CB00010B/1465